Published by
KELSEY PUBLISHING LTD

Printed in Singapore by Stamford Press PTE Ltd.
on behalf of
Kelsey Publishing Ltd,
Cudham Tithe Barn,
Berry's Hill,
Cudham,
Kent TN16 3AG
Tel: 01959 541444
Fax: 01959 541400
E-mail: kelseybooks@kelsey.co.uk

© 1999
ISBN 1 873098 51 0

Acknowledgements
Our thanks go to Chris Graham who wrote this Electronic Diagnostics series and also to the expert assistance
provided by Frank Massey of Fuel Injection Services, Keith Derbyshire at Sykes-Pickavant,
Richard Keys at ATP Electronic Developments Ltd, Simon Ashby of Diagnostic Techniques and Charles White of Equiptech.

INTRODUCTION

Welcome to another volume of *Car Mechanics'* highly popular Electronic Diagnostics series. For those of you who are not familiar with the feature, every month we take a detailed look at a particular model's electronics; identifying familiar faults and suggesting the suitable solution. We'll also point out the special tools needed and the relevant test procedures required to resolve those annoying electronic niggles.

It's our way of demystifying the whole electronics side of the modern motor car. And as cars become more and more complex, so the dependence on ECUs becomes greater. This series therefore makes a great ally if you spend a lot of time working on this area of the car, particularly if you're in the trade. In this volume we tackle some of the more popular modern applications such as: Ford's EEC V system – as used on their latest models; Vauxhall's Bosch Motronic unit; VW's Seimans system – as used on their superb turbo diesel; Renault's Fenix 5 set-up and the ever-popular Mini, now fitted with MEMS 2J engine management.

And as security is such a big issue with modern cars, there's a chapter in this book that takes a look at modern electronic immobilisers. This is particularly useful because of the number of cars on the roads these days that use these systems, be it a keypad activated unit or a chip within the ignition key. Either way, they can be a pain when they go wrong, and this piece aims to help remove those grey areas on the subject.
As usual, Chris Graham has researched this subject tirelessly, with the able assistance of Frank Massey, from Preston-based Fuel Injection Services, and Simon Ashby from Diagnostic Techniques, who are based in Reading. Both are highly knowledgeable on the subject of electronic diagnostics and continue to serve us well.

As more new models are launched, so these electronic systems develop and evolve, which means that there is plenty more scope left in the series. So we'll continue to run these articles every month in *Car Mechanics*, and in time we will build them up to form another indispensable guide to electronic diagnostics. I think we'll call it *Car Mechanics* Electronic Diagnostics Volume 4!

Phil Weeden
Editor

ELECTRONIC DIAGNOSTICS – INDEX

PREPARATION

SUPPLEMENT

IMMOBILISERS

SYSTEMS

ELECTRONIC DIAGNOSTICS – INDEX (cont'd)

CONTENTS

ELECTRONIC DIAGNOSTICS!

Tracing and fixing faults in electronic engine management systems

Number 41: The stylish-looking Citroën Xantia is a popular seller, but what about its workshop manners? Chris Graham finds out more.

Citroën's attractive Xantia is around in great numbers now and, by and large, has a good reputation in all respects. Setting aside the newly-introduced V6 version, secondhand buyers have the choice between eight and 16-valve engines and we've picked a late 2.0 8v to examine this month.

Frank Massey, proprietor at electronic tuning specialist Fuel Injection

POSSIBLE FAULTS
1. **MoT failure**
2. **Rich mixture**
3. **Over-fuelling**

Services (Tel: 01772 201597) is a big fan of the Magneti Marelli 8P total engine management system which runs the show. The same system is used by Peugeot as well, on 8v models in the

106, 306 and 405 ranges.

For those in any doubt about the system fitted, and there have been many versions since its introduction, the designers have conveniently marked a reference number on the ECU casing. A three-digit number, at the end of a lengthy sequence of numbers, precisely denotes the software version fitted (notable examples include 004, 012, 124 etc).

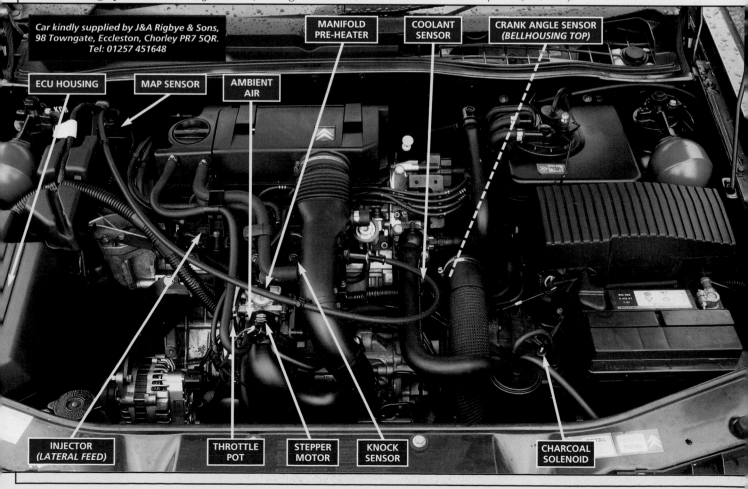

Car kindly supplied by J&A Rigbye & Sons, 98 Towngate, Eccleston, Chorley PR7 5QR. Tel: 01257 451648

MANIFOLD PRE-HEATER

COOLANT SENSOR

CRANK ANGLE SENSOR (BELLHOUSING TOP)

ECU HOUSING

MAP SENSOR

AMBIENT AIR

INJECTOR (LATERAL FEED)

THROTTLE POT

STEPPER MOTOR

KNOCK SENSOR

CHARCOAL SOLENOID

ENGINE MANAGEMENT

This system provides complete engine management and the primary components included consist of: a crank angle sensor at the back of the bell housing; a traditional coolant temperature sensor at the back of the thermostat housing (awkward to get at) on the n/s of the engine; an ambient air sensor in the throttle housing near the pre-heater; a throttle position sensor which is a potentiometer type, not a switch; an external MAP sensor for assessing engine load fitted on the o/s of the car on a bulk-head-mounted bracket.

There is a pezio-ceramic knock sensor at the front of the block; four laterally-fed fuel injectors; a four-wire stepper valve for regulating the idle speed controlled directly by the ECU; a charcoal canister, at the front n/s of the engine bay, for absorbing HC emissions from the fuel tank and releasing them into the engine under cer-

tain conditions; a road speed sensor – input from the gearbox.

There is a composite relay mounted next to the ECU on the o/s of the engine bay at the front. One half comprises the power-up circuits for the ECU while the other provides the fuel pump pull down. Also there is an intake manifold pre-heater, although these are not always fitted on multipoint applications. This is powered by the same fuse-controlled circuit which controls the oxygen sensor – found in the exhaust downpipe as usual.

The system operates with a DIS ignition system. There is a dual coil pack and each plug is fed directly. There is no distributor cap with traditional king lead or rotor arm. The coil pack is controlled directly by the ECU – there is no separate module involved in this case. Trigger signals are internally generated within the control unit.

There is a diagnostic socket in the driver's footwell, although this is a fairly unusual type. It is unique to the Xantia, and the pic here shows the Sykes-Pickavant connector kit which has been specifically designed for the purpose.

The system is code-readable. Serial data can be accessed and many actuators can be driven for test and assessment purposes. Components which can be operated include charcoal canister, injectors, fuel pump etc. Injection duration time can be studied too.

The engine features a composite (non-metal) manifold. Frank considers the system overall to be a very good one. Drivability and reliability are generally good but the biggest single problem with these cars – and similar Citroën models – relates to getting them through the fast idle test in the MoT test.

PREPARATION

The good news on the preparation front is that, in most cases, none will be required. This engine doesn't exhibit any dirty habits, remains generally oil-free and is well-mannered in all respects. Frank has yet to come across any significant or inherent wiring problems to worry about and has nothing but praise for the quality of the installation from an electronics point of view.

Generally you will find very little debris or contamination collected in the intake system and Frank reports that he has never yet needed to remove a stepper motor for cleaning. Spark plug access is reasonable so it's worth whipping these out for a visual check. The leads are normally of good quality and rarely suffer from electrical tracking problems. Cast an eye over them for obvious damage nonetheless.

If cheap non-original equipment leads have been fitted, then the chances are that sub-standard plugs have been specified too. Change these for o/e quality products before doing anything else.

FAULT SORTING

The first fault, that of MoT test failure is a strange one indeed. It's more of a technicality than a fault, but can result in a hefty bill for the owner nevertheless. The problem is one of emissions, and the way in which the car is tested.

No deterioration in performance will be noticeable but at the time of the test an emissions check failure, specifically in relation to the Lambda reading, will cause the vehicle to fail. Frank says that these cars actually run lean. The MoT station looks at just two gases, CO and HC, and uses these to

calculate a theoretical Lambda reading. Normally, a high oxygen content is shown but this is not because the engine is under-fuelling. If you check with a four-gas analyser they are only marginally lean but this slightly higher oxygen content is enough to make it fail. Frank thinks this is ridiculous, particularly as oxygen is not a pollutant.

Unfortunately, because the resultant Lambda value is out of spec, the car fails. It should be between 0.97-1.03% (lambda) at fast idle. Many of these cars show 1.1 – ie just fractionally over the 1.03 and, unfortunately, to cure them can be an involved business.

The first port of call should be the software version being used by the ECU. There have been about eight software updates since the introduction of the 8P system and this is an on-going process. It needs to be version 124 or higher to ensure a test pass

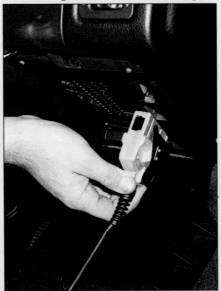

This is the special plug needed to connect the Sykes-Pickavant Advanced Code Reader to the Xantia's diagnostic socket. It is unique to this application.

these days. Anything lower than this is unlikely to be able to reach the latest standards so, unfortunately, the ECU will have to be swapped.

The problem is complicated by the fact that not every car fails the test, and those that do don't all do it in the same manner! This makes the repair method that much more difficult.

The operation of the oxygen sensor is obviously essential as well. Check that it is switching at a frequency of one hertz or better, with a full switching range of 200-800mV. Also make sure that the heater circuit for the sensor is functioning and powered up with a full 12V supply. The earth reference for the Lambda sensor can quite often be less than perfect, according to Frank. Sometimes it may be higher than it should be (say 0.5V) or it might suffer with electrical 'noise'. By directly wiring the earth to the vehicle's battery, which is conveniently close at hand, the switching will almost always be improved. If this is the case then 'hard wire' the sensor in this way and leave it as a permanent fixture.

If the Lambda switch is still poor, but not being caused by a fuelling error, then swap the sensor for a new one. It is important to get this part right first. Then re-evaluate the exhaust gas content at the tailpipe. If the lambda value is still high then you are looking at a software upgrade to a more recent version.

Replacement ECUs from the dealer cost about £400, but units can be rebuilt with the latest specification software for about £175 by specialist dealer network agents through ATP (Tel: 01543 467466). Remember that you can't casually swap ECUs between cars because of the security coding.

The other factor to bear in mind is that the exhaust is in tip-top condition.

ELECTRONIC DIAGNOSTICS!

Holes anywhere in the system will cause chaos. If there is even just a slight hole present the car will not fail at idle because neither the HC or the CO levels would be dramatically effected.

Because the car continues to drive so well even with the presence of this condition, Frank does not really describe it as a fault as such. It is only the slightly high oxygen content which is driving up the Lambda value and leading to the test failure.

Another relatively common problem associated with the 8v Xantia concerns fuelling mixture. Sometimes if a car is left to idle for a while, say five minutes, this may trigger the mixture to go rich and the engine might stall. It will usually re-start, but gives the impression of being flooded. Inspecting the plugs at this stage will show them to be sooty.

The root of this problem is the charcoal canister. As we know, this is a device designed to absorb excess hydrocarbons from the fuel tank, to hold them and then, at an appropriate time, to release them into the engine. This usually happens to provide cold start enrichment or under conditions of hard acceleration.

The supply from the canister is controlled by a solenoid valve and herein lies the problem. If its action becomes faulty several things can happen. One possibility is that actual fuel is drawn through the valve and into the canister – normally this should be restricted to vapour only. Frank had one example recently where fuel was being drawn directly into the engine in this way, which caused the mixture to go very rich. The Lambda sensor, in a bid to control the situation, instructed the injectors to 'lean off' the mixture and the engine ran very badly as a consequence.

To isolate this as the cause of the problem the simplest course of action is to remove the pipe which runs from the canister to the inlet manifold. Run the car with this supply pipe blanked off and check whether the fault re-occurs. If it doesn't then you can as-

The external MAP sensor is bracket-mounted and so easily inspected if needs be.

TECHNICAL SPECIFICATIONS

ECU PIN	COMPONENT	VALUE
1/19	Ignition CB pulse	CB waveform
2/3, 20/21	Idle valve signal	12V digital
22	Carbon canister	12v digital
27	Speed sensor (vehicle)	12v digital
28	Crank angle sensor output:	
	cranking	2V+ A/C
	idle	12V+ A/C
11/17	CAS earth and sensor return	
29	Oxygen sensor output	200-800mV @ 1Hz+
30	Throttle pos indicator output:	
	throttle closed	0.3-0.5V
	throttle open	4.5V
14	TPi ECU supply (shared)	5V
16	TPi earth	0.25V
13	Coolant sensor output:	
	cold	3-3.5V
	hot	1V
17	CS earth (shared)	0.25V
31	Ambient air sensor	3V/20°C
16	AAS earth (shared)	0.25V
32	MAP sensor output:	
	static	3.5V
	idle	1.6V
14	MAP ECU supply (shared)	5V
16	MAP earth (shared)	0.25V
33	Knock sensor - active	0.5-1V at 15KHz
16	KS earth return (shared)	0.25V
18	Injector durations:	
	cold cranking	8ms
	hot cranking	5ms
	cold idle	5ms
	hot idle	3ms
	snap (hot)	8-12ms

(injectors have saturated pulse, intermittent control)

sume that the canister is saturated with fuel. Frank's advice is to remove it, invert it to remove any excess and then allow it time to dry out naturally. As an extra precaution it may be wise to replace the solenoid control valve in case the seat of the original has rusted or become stuck.

Frank thinks that this problem is unlikely to be caused by the control end of things at the ECU and is most likely to be a physical problem which can be dealt with by component replacement.

Continuing on the same fuelling theme, another relatively common problem with this application is one of permanent over-fuelling. A recent case of this to pass through Frank's hands showed that the problem was confined to one cylinder only.

All the normal checks were carried out and nothing out of the ordinary appeared. Injector duration was about right, coolant sensor output was correct, the MAP sensor signal was fine too. The fuel pressure was correct but the Lambda sensor switching rate confirmed the presence of a rich mixture – it was set permanently to 'go lean'.

The most basic check of all, a close inspection of the spark plugs, highlighted over-fuelling in one cylinder. The problem, in fact, related to the injector after all. Being laterally-fed, each injector is surrounded by fuel. Two seals – upper and lower – keep this fuel where it should be and it was the lower one which was leaking. This was allowing fuel to enter the engine in an uncontrolled manner so over-fuelling was the result. There was no external sign that this was happening.

This problem can relate to the bad fitting of injectors. The sealing rings can become crimped or damaged by careless treatment and so the problem goes unnoticed until the symptoms present themselves. Frank has also heard stories about the composite manifolds cracking. This, of course, will also allow extra fuel into the engine.

As far as the injector sealing rings are concerned, examination will have to be a careful one because the split or cut may be very small. If in any doubt, replace the seals, and replace the injectors carefully with the aid of a silicone-based lubricant spray. Incidentally, while the injectors are out of the car, it

11

Check ECU case label if in doubt about software version being used.

makes sense to get them tested on a flow bench to double-check for sticking or dribbling.

In theory, Frank says that it should be possible to detect this fault with the use of a fuel pressure gauge. Attach it to the fuel rail, run the engine and then switch off. The fuel pressure will drop initially but then should be retained at about 1.5 bar – it normally runs at about 2.5 bar. The residual pressure should then be held for a long time, so if it bleeds off rapidly, then clearly the fuel is leaking out somewhere.

In this instance, however, and knowing the system as he does, Frank feels happy to remove the injectors straightaway as this is most often the cause. Replacement seals are easy to fit but harder to obtain. Frank suspects that most dealers will try to sell a complete injector rather than supply just the O-ring seals for a few pence. You will need to seek out an independent component specialist (give Frank a call for a contact) for the necessary bits.

NEXT MONTH
Vauxhall Astra 1.4i

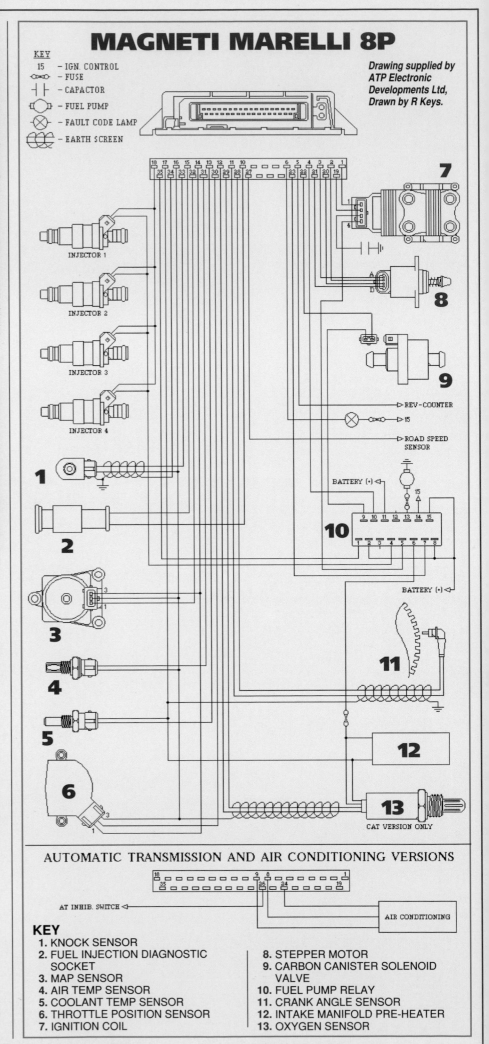

MAGNETI MARELLI 8P

KEY
15 – IGN. CONTROL
– FUSE
– CAPACTOR
– FUEL PUMP
– FAULT CODE LAMP
– EARTH SCREEN

Drawing supplied by ATP Electronic Developments Ltd, Drawn by R Keys.

REV-COUNTER
15
ROAD SPEED SENSOR
BATTERY (+)
15
BATTERY (+)
CAT VERSION ONLY

AUTOMATIC TRANSMISSION AND AIR CONDITIONING VERSIONS

AT INHIB. SWITCH

AIR CONDITIONING

KEY
1. KNOCK SENSOR
2. FUEL INJECTION DIAGNOSTIC SOCKET
3. MAP SENSOR
4. AIR TEMP SENSOR
5. COOLANT TEMP SENSOR
6. THROTTLE POSITION SENSOR
7. IGNITION COIL
8. STEPPER MOTOR
9. CARBON CANISTER SOLENOID VALVE
10. FUEL PUMP RELAY
11. CRANK ANGLE SENSOR
12. INTAKE MANIFOLD PRE-HEATER
13. OXYGEN SENSOR

ELECTRONIC DIAGNOSTICS!

Tracing and fixing faults in electronic engine management systems

Number 42: *The evergreen Astra 1.4i is a willing worker and popular fleet vehicle. But what of its management manners? Chris Graham digs deep to find out.*

Vauxhall's latest engine management system for its small-engined models is called Multec. It is available in a variety of guises but the one we are dealing with here is denoted 'M', standing for multipoint. There is also a singlepoint version identified – yes, you've guessed it, 'S'!

Multec is GM's own system and it provides complete engine manage-

POSSIBLE FAULTS
1. **CAS failure**
2. **Lambda sensor**
3. **'Limp home'**

ment – fuelling and ignition control. There are a couple of possible ignition set-ups available, either a standard system with coil and conventional distributor cap and rotor arm, or a DIS

'wasted spark' alternative. The car featured here adopts the traditional coil-based approach.

Multec is also found on other 1.4-engined models, including Novas and Corsas, together with 1.6 litre versions of the Cavalier, Astra and Tigra, plus some 1.8 litre Cavalier applications. All feature closed-loop emission control systems and a diagnostic socket, providing access to blink codes and the

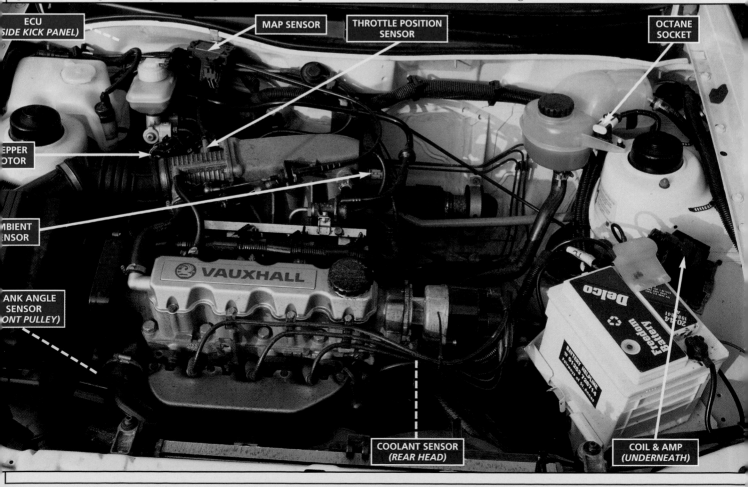

ECU (SIDE KICK PANEL)

MAP SENSOR

THROTTLE POSITION SENSOR

OCTANE SOCKET

STEPPER MOTOR

AMBIENT SENSOR

CRANK ANGLE SENSOR (FRONT PULLEY)

COOLANT SENSOR (REAR HEAD)

COIL & AMP (UNDERNEATH)

ENGINE MANAGEMENT

There is no main relay to power up this system, instead this is achieved by an ignition-fed supply. The fuel pump is relay-governed, and this is controlled directly by the ECU so there is a safety function there too.

Major components in this Multec-M system consist of: a crank angle sensor mounted externally on the front pulley in a vulnerable position down by the front off-side wheel; a road speed sensor built into the speedometer head rather than within the gearbox; and a MAP sensor which acts as the engine load device and is found on the engine bulkhead.

There is a coolant temperature sensor at the back of the cylinder head, a standard two-wire, NTC component; an air temperature sensor sited at the back of the inlet manifold, again a two-wire NTC unit;

and a single-wire Lambda (oxygen) sensor which is not heated and relies on heat from the exhaust gas to bring it up to temperature.

In addition, there is an external four-wire ignition amplifier module under the coil. This receives a trigger from the ECU before it, in turn, switches the coil. There are four fuel injectors mounted in a conventional fuel rail, all being controlled by a fuel pressure regulator. There is a stepper motor to control engine idle speed; a throttle position sensor; a diagnostic socket found behind a trim panel below and to the right of the steering wheel; an octane adjust socket found on the nearside inner wing, towards the rear of the engine bay – this alters the ignition timing for different types of fuel.

If the speedometer cable is disconnected (or breaks!), the engine management system will be thrown into 'limp home' mode and normal engine performance will be lost. This is because the road speed sensor will have been detached.

Very unusually, the coolant temperature sensor has a dual range. It starts with an output of about 2.5V when cold, and gradually decreases to around 1.2V as it warms. Then it suddenly rises to 3V, followed by a slight decrease to 2.5V or so when the engine is fully hot. Frank does not know of any other system where the coolant sensor performs in this way. He says that GM argue that it affords greater control but wonders, if that's so, why no other manufacturers adopt the same approach!

---

ability to drive actuators and gather serial data using a code reader.

It should be noted that there is a variety of subtly different components used across the Multec system range. Frank Massey, our experienced electronics guide and founder of Preston-based Fuel Injection Services (Tel: 01772 201597) explains that there are three different types of signal generator available. These vital components, which trigger the whole system, can take the form of: an inductive pick-up built in to the distributor; a Hall effect generator, also found in the distributor; or a conventional crank angle sensor.

The Astra here is fitted with a crank angle sensor, but Frank stresses that, in general tuning terms, the signal generator type makes little difference to basic diagnostic operations. The behaviour and voltage pattern of each only varies slightly so, unless there is a specific problem with the generator itself, it need not concern you.

Overall, Frank considers this Multec system to be pretty good in terms of reliability and performance. There are certainly a few inherent problems likely to occur, but none is very serious. The whole installation is easy to work on, with an excellent, roomy layout making for speedy, straightforward progress.

PREPARATION

This is not at all a bad system in terms of dirt ingress and general contamination levels. Nevertheless, the obvious factors still need to be checked. The area around the plugs quite often collects road dirt, so wash this away carefully. Be sure, too, that the plugs fitted are the right ones (correct heat range) and that the gaps are set accurately.

The rotor arm and distributor cap internals suffer in the usual way and should be inspected. Remove the cap,

check electrode condition, wash and dry thoroughly. Also clean and dry the plug leads carefully to avoid the risk of electrical tracking.

Generally, as far as wiring is concerned, there are no major problem areas, apart from contamination of the crank angle sensor – we'll deal with this later on – and the distributor generator socket (when fitted).

The air intake system doesn't suffer too badly either, but it never hurts to wash out the pipework and check the cleanliness of the throttle disc and body. Frank says that he has yet to find it necessary to remove and wash an idle control valve on this application.

The only other significant point to check is the condition of the MAP sensor pipe. This runs between the sensor and the intake manifold and its integrity is vital to the correct functioning of the management system. Look for kinks and splits in the pipe, and also check that it has not become 'soggy' due to an ingress of oil. Thankfully, this pipe is positioned well and runs in a predominantly straight line. The MAP sensor is located at a high

point too, so any fluid in the pipe tends to drain back down into the engine, which is fine.

PINNING DOWN PROBLEMS

Perhaps the most common fault to afflict this Vauxhall Astra application is intermittent crank angle sensor failure. This will lead directly to all sorts of drivability problems, including misfiring.

As we mentioned earlier, the sensor is located low down on the offside of the vehicle, close to the front wheel. Consequently, it does suffer with general contamination and, if this is allowed to build up, then problems will result. The output signal will be affected. The 'shape' of the signal is determined by a phonic wheel, which is mounted to the front pulley. This too can become contaminated with dirt,

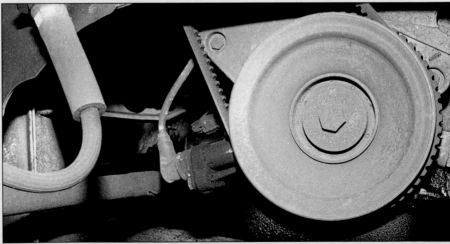

To the left of the main pulley is the bracket-mounted crank angle sensor (CAS). This takes its input from the phonic wheel, which is fixed to the rear of the pulley, the castellated edge of which can just be seen down the right-hand side of the pulley here.

ELECTRONIC DIAGNOSTICS!

with similarly destructive results.

In most cases any contamination can be removed from the 'castellated' phonic wheel with a wire brush. The wheel is mounted on the outside edge of the front pulley and so is completely exposed to the elements. In addition, it can be prone to damage as well, which Frank has often seen.

If the front pulley has to be removed (during a timing belt change for example) and a lever is used to help with this, then the phonic wheel is very easily damaged. Frank says that it needs only to be distorted by a few thousandths of an inch for the profile of the signal to be destroyed – it really is that sensitive. The only solution is to use a quality puller so force is applied in a controlled manner!

Damage and distortion to the phonic wheel alters the air gap between it and the sensor, and this is the crucial factor. Small variations in the gap will be sufficient to throw the signal out of specification, making it unrecognisable to the ECU and leading to a fault being registered. The consequences of this can be that the engine will fail to run at all, or the management system will be thrown into default mode, leading to very 'flat' performance or misfires.

In its original form, the sensor had a steel body and was mounted in an alloy housing. Consequently, corrosion sets in between the two and eventually acts to crush the sensor, leading to intermittent breakdown. Failure most commonly takes place on a heat-related basis. As the assembly warms up, the components expand and the sensor is crushed and performance is lost. As it cools, the pressure is relieved and so the correct output is returned.

Problems with this sensor should normally be traceable through the fault code system but this, of course, will give no clue about the nature of the fault. The sure-fire method is to test the output signal with an oscilloscope. In fact, problems, in the early stages, will only be picked up by a scope – they will be too quick to trigger the fault code.

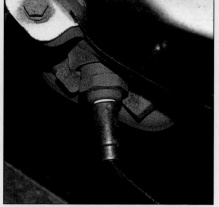

The single-wire Lambda sensor on this Astra application can suffer with a poor earth, the path for which is via the exhaust system.

If you suspect the CAS is at fault, then make sure you replace it with the new version, which has sensibly been housed in a plastic body. The original metal sensors were made by Bosch, while the more recent versions are by Siemens.

Because the Lambda sensor used on this application is a single-wire component, it makes its earth connection

COMPONENT CATALOGUE

A new 1998 product catalogue will be made available from ATP Electronic Developments Ltd during January. It lists an extensive range of re-manufactured electronic control units and air flow meters. Copies can be secured by faxing your address details to ATP on 01543 467426.

through its body and then the car's exhaust system. With age, the reference of this earth can rise, which can lead to problems, including poor drivability and MoT test failure. The system may even be thrown into 'limp home' mode but, whatever happens, the throttle response will certainly become poor.

In Frank's experience, the performance if these sensors in general is superb. Commonly he finds them switching at five Hertz or more once warm, which is excellently active. Occasionally, however, contamination and rusting around the sensor and on the exhaust mean that the earth reference becomes poor and the all-important switching action becomes slow or non-existent.

In such cases it is important to realise that simply switching with a new component may not be the complete answer because it is being screwed back into exactly the same exhaust system. If you find that a new sensor is still not switching as it should, Frank suggests that a modified sensor is fitted. He says these are available independently and can be multi-wired units.

This gives you the flexibility to instate a heater circuit (powered through the fuel pump relay) if you wish but, more importantly, allows for a separate earth to be connected. This can be connected to the battery earth or any other suitable point and should solve the switching problem at a stroke. Another piece of good news is that Lambda sensor prices have virtually halved in recent times. Now Frank says that quality components can be secured for about £75 each.

Finally, Frank has come across a number of examples where cars appear to be stuck in 'limp home' mode for no apparent reason. Often this can be accompanied by an idle speed of about 1,200rpm. While the engine will drive reasonably well, the over-run fuel cut off function is lost and so fuel economy tends to suffer as well. There is no adjustment potential for the engine idle speed – it is all computer controlled.

The cause of this is usually that the speedometer cable has been disconnected for some reason and this is logged by the ECU as a fault with the road speed sensor. Even if the cable and sensor are connected back again the fault tends not to clear and the vehicle is left in permanent 'limp home' mode.

TECHNICAL SPECIFICATIONS

COMPONENT	OUTPUT	ECU PIN
Crank angle sensor		
Cranking	4V peak to peak	A2
Idle	8V peak to peak	
Cruise (3k)	12V peak to peak	
Road speed sensor	12V digital	B2
MAP sensor	Atmos 4.7V	A7
	Idle	1.7V
Coolant temp sensor		
Cold	2.5V	B12
Intermediate low value	1.2V	
Hot	2.25V	
Air temp sensor		
20°C	2.25V	D3
Lambda sensor	0.2-0.8V at 5Hz+	B11
Ign module trigger	12V digital	D10
Throttle pos indicator		
Closed	0.5V	A8
Open	4.5V	
Idle control valve	12V digital	C5/6-C8/9
Fuel injectors		
Cold crank	10+ms	C10 (cyl 1+2)
Cold idle	3ms	
Hot crank	4+ms	C11 (cyl 3+4)
Hot idle	1.5ms	
(current-controlled pulse)		
Octane plug		
95 octane	1VD11	
98 octane	1.6V	

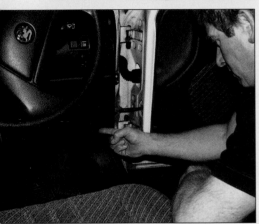

Gaining access to the ECU is a little tricky. It is tucked away behind this kick panel. When you reach it, Frank advises the use of a breakout box, explaining that 'back-probing' is tricky because of the 'tightness' of the terminations – it's hard to be precise.

The problem is compounded by the fact that no warning light will show on the dash. This will certainly be illuminated while the sensor is disconnected but, once the connection is re-established, the light will go out even though the fault still remains logged.

The only solution, according to Frank, is to disconnect the negative terminal at the battery and re-activate the 'block learn' system. Leave this disconnected for about 30 seconds then reconnect and drive the car around for 10-15 minutes. After this all systems should have re-set themselves back to the pre-programmed factory specification and all will be well from then on.

An identical problem can arise if the throttle potentiometer is disconnected and then plugged in again. The idle speed will remain at 1,200rpm until you take the system through the block learn process again. This cannot be done with a code reader, it has to be achieved by powering down the ECU.

If this does not do the trick, and the road speed sensor and the throttle pot are both OK, the most likely cause is an air leak somewhere else in the system.

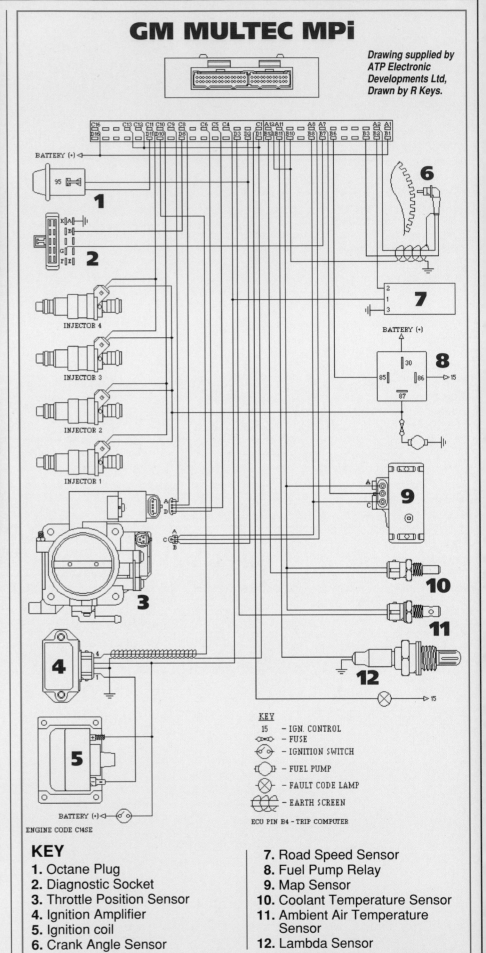

GM MULTEC MPi

Drawing supplied by ATP Electronic Developments Ltd, Drawn by R Keys.

KEY
15 – IGN. CONTROL
– FUSE
– IGNITION SWITCH
– FUEL PUMP
– FAULT CODE LAMP
– EARTH SCREEN
ECU PIN B4 - TRIP COMPUTER

ENGINE CODE C14SE

KEY

1. Octane Plug
2. Diagnostic Socket
3. Throttle Position Sensor
4. Ignition Amplifier
5. Ignition coil
6. Crank Angle Sensor
7. Road Speed Sensor
8. Fuel Pump Relay
9. Map Sensor
10. Coolant Temperature Sensor
11. Ambient Air Temperature Sensor
12. Lambda Sensor

NEXT MONTH
Ford Fiesta 1.25 (EEC V)

ELECTRONIC DIAGNOSTICS!

Tracing and fixing faults in electronic engine management systems

Number 43: We take our first look at Ford's state-of-the-art management system, EEC V, as found on the Fiesta 1.25. Chris Graham reports.

Despite having been around for some two years now, technical information on Ford's EEC V engine management package remains thin on the ground. So, in a bid to spill the beans for Car Mechanics readers, Frank Massey, electronics expert at Fuel Injection Services (Tel: 01772 201597), rolled up his sleeves, sharpened his probe, and set about interrogating an unsuspecting Fiesta.

POSSIBLE PROBLEMS
1. Fast idle
2. Poor running
3. CAS failure

The EEC V system represents a significant enhancement over the previous EEC IV version. One of the fundamental differences between the two is that 'five' uses a much more sophis-

ticated electronic control unit, with 104 pin connectors as opposed to 60. It has also adopted the OBD2-style, 16-pin diagnostic socket. The significance of this is that it creates problems from a diagnostics point of view. Only a few independent manufacturers of serial diagnostic equipment produce compatible hardware, so prices are high.

However, as with all management systems, there is always the option of

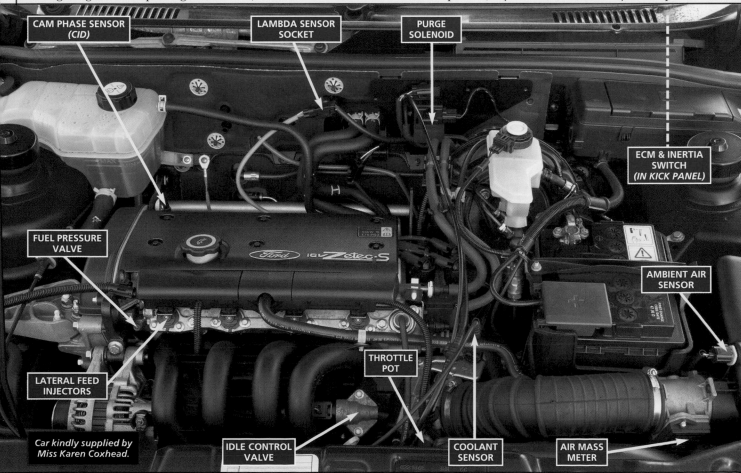

CAM PHASE SENSOR (CID)

LAMBDA SENSOR SOCKET

PURGE SOLENOID

ECM & INERTIA SWITCH (IN KICK PANEL)

FUEL PRESSURE VALVE

AMBIENT AIR SENSOR

LATERAL FEED INJECTORS

THROTTLE POT

Car kindly supplied by Miss Karen Coxhead.

IDLE CONTROL VALVE

COOLANT SENSOR

AIR MASS METER

ENGINE MANAGEMENT

This EEC V system is reasonably straight-forward. It provides total engine management through a single ECU which is mounted behind the n/s kick panel. The car featured here was also fitted with a metal cover over the ECU which Frank believes is a security device. It was pop-riveted into place, and he assumes its purpose is to make theft of the unit more difficult. There is no technical reason for its inclusion.

The system runs on multipoint, sequential fuel injection – one injector per cylinder, each being individually controlled directly by the ECU. The injectors are laterally-fed components and it should be noted that the engine now makes use of a composite inlet manifold. Frank believes that apart from saving weight, these 'plastic' manifolds are more thermally efficient too.

Major components consist of: an idle control valve; a Lambda sensor (fitted very conveniently at the top of the exhaust manifold at the rear of the engine); and a 'wasted spark' ignition system with double-ended coil directly controlled from the ECU (there is no EDIS module as used to be used).

There is an inertia switch to defeat the fuel pump in the event of an impact (next to the ECU); a charcoal canister with an 'evap' control valve for dealing with HC emissions from the fuel tank; and a crankshaft sensor at the back of the flywheel, near the bell housing, which provides the key 'trigger' input for the whole system; a camshaft sensor (CID) at the top of the camshaft housing at the rear of the engine.

Also, there is a coolant temperature sensor found close to the thermostat housing at the rear of the engine; an intake air temperature sensor located in the air box; an air mass flow meter; a throttle position sensor on the end of the throttle shaft; a clutch pedal switch for enhanced engine stall control; a power steering switch for the same purpose; and an octane adjustment plug.

Finally, there is an in-tank fuel pump feeding a composite fuel rail surrounding the injectors, and controlled by a pressure regulator; a fuel pump relay; and a vehicle speed sensor.

This car is also fitted with a PATS (Passive Anti-Theft System) alarm which makes use of a dual encrypted ignition key. Basically there are two codes, one on the key fob and the other in the ECU, which must agree before the engine can be started. Critical control systems within the engine are disabled when the alarm is set. Possible problems can arise if the key becomes corrupted, at which point the vehicle will have to be returned to the dealer for re-encryption. Copy keys can be encrypted by owners from the 'master' key, but if the latter is lost or damaged the dealer provides the only possible solution.

investigating the system using a break-out box, and this, in general, is the method which Frank favours anyway. Coincidentally, equipment specialist Autodiagnos (Tel: 01772 887774) have just released a brand new break-out box specifically for EEC V applications.

The beauty of the break-out box approach is that it is connected between the ECU and the vehicle's wiring loom, to provide easy and convenient access to all pins. Unfortunately, this equipment is not cheap either. The break-out box itself costs about £400, but added to this is the cost of the connection device which boosts the total cost to about £800. The layout and close proximity of pins on this type of modern ECU is very restrictive. So much so that the old-fashioned method of back-probing can no longer be regarded as a practical proposition.

The break-out box provides a window through which you can view any signals passing in or out of the ECU. This provides a significant advantage over 'serial diagnostics' which is essentially the viewing of logged fault codes stored within the ECU. Remember that fault codes represent only what the ECU is theoretically 'seeing' and can be at odds with what is actually happening. Using 'parallel diagnostics' (with a break-out box) presents the whole picture as it actually is. You are dealing with the real signal so there can be no dispute.

The other problem with serial communication is that the component will only be logged as faulty if and when it begins to operate out of specification. Running out of range can cause just as many problems but will not always trigger the appropriate fault code.

There is no lamp on the dash to warn the driver of an engine management problem, and Frank does not agree with this omission. Also, because the 'limp home' mode is so efficient now, there is a very real risk that problems will arise without the driver being aware that anything is wrong at all, which can compound the faults and increase the rectification costs unnecessarily.

PREPARATION

The engine bay layout on this Fiesta is very impressive. There is plenty of room, and access to all major components is easy. There is a large plastic cover, which protects the top of the engine and the HT leads. While this is largely a cosmetic addition, Frank believes that it will also stop most dirt and debris reaching the plug apertures which is good.

Nevertheless, he still thinks it worthwhile to remove the cover and carry out a visual inspection of the whole area. Remove the HT leads and check the apertures for contamination of any sort. Wash and dry the leads. There should be few problems with these, as

This is the metal plate which is pop riveted over the ECU, presumably as a security precaution. The black box on top of the ECU is the Autodiagnos interface unit (A020247/1) which provides the break-out box with electrical access to the entire system.

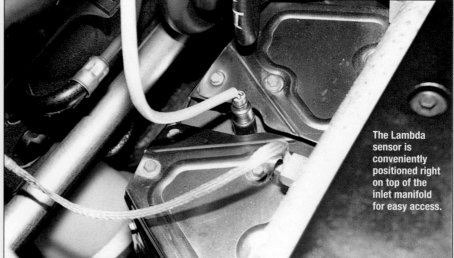

The Lambda sensor is conveniently positioned right on top of the inlet manifold for easy access.

ELECTRONIC DIAGNOSTICS!

Plug leads on this application of are the 'sealed in rubber' variety and are generally very reliable. Nevertheless, problems can arise with electrical tracking, so clean and check them carefully.

they are fully enclosed in rubber, but Frank has come across a couple of examples where brand new ones have been faulty – leading to tracking. Check the plugs carefully – these should be platinum electrode components.

The air intake into the throttle body is again easy to get to and doesn't normally suffer too badly. However, wash it out to clear any carbon that may have built up around the throttle disc. Likewise, the idle control valve, which is easy to access at the front of the block, should be removed so that the active components can be washed. Lightly lubricate before re-assembling.

Apart from this, there is nothing else to worry about. Frank is not aware of any characteristic problems in terms of components shaking loose or wiring chafing, but then he admits that it is still early days yet. However, he remains optimistic, because the whole installation appears so neat, well routed and securely clipped.

The EEC V management system is still relatively new and so, accordingly, Frank has come across few serious, inherent problems yet. However, making some educated guesses based on experience and the performance of recent Ford applications, he has highlighted what he considers are some potential trouble spots.

The first of these is the throttle potentiometer. On earlier Zetec engines the pot was often found to be sticking with the effect that the throttle was held slightly open, causing a high engine idle. Alternatively, it might also cause the idle valve to be isolated, and thus engine stalling becomes a problem.

The root of the trouble was a sealing washer within the component which became distorted and caused the 'sticky' action. Unfortunately, the internals of the pot cannot be lubricated because they need to be completely clean to function correctly. Replacement is the simplest solution but Frank always thinks it wise to try some very light lubrication – WD40 or a silicone-based lubricant on the spindle – as a first move.

Another possibility with this application relates to the battery. If you have been working on a car and find

that, once the job has been finished it tends to run badly, then don't automatically assume the worst. The first question to ask is whether or not the battery has been disconnected.

If the power supply has been disconnected, for whatever reason, the 'keep alive memory' within the ECU will be lost. The same thing can be caused if the KAM fuse blows. Modern applications like EEC V feature 'block learn', also known as 'adaptive memory', which means that they monitor inputs through various sensors and adapt or learn from these, so that engine running and performance remains largely constant as the vehicle ages. For example, if the idle control valve is being held continually open for some reason then eventually this will become accepted by the ECU as being the correct position. It will be adopted as the norm and will be stored as such.

If the battery is disconnected then all this stored information is lost and it must be 're-learned'. Putting this right is simply a matter of driving the car for about 10 miles, under varying road conditions. The same effect can strike

if you have replaced a component, such as the Lambda sensor or throttle pot, with a new one. The system will be 'block learned' to the performance of the old one, which may have been sluggish in operation, or even faulty. So under these conditions, and before checking emissions, it would be wise to re-instate the block learn process by pulling the KAM fuse and then driving the car. After this you can re-assess the condition of the vehicle.

Another worthwhile component for special consideration, particularly as vehicles start to age, is the crank angle sensor. Cars used around town a lot, or maybe for driving instruction, can suffer with a build-up of clutch dust in the bell housing. While this is not a desperate problem in itself, it must be remembered that the critical sensor for the whole EEC V system, the crank angle sensor, is found in this region too – and it is magnetic!

Metallic dust and debris is attracted readily to this component, and build up of this can have a detrimental effect. The signal from the CAS is absolutely crucial, as is its profile. Fluctuations resulting from contamination will often lead to engine misfires, erratic running, or even stalling. If you find that the signal is at fault – and this will have to be checked using an oscilloscope – Frank advises that it is well worth removing and cleaning the sensor first, before opting to replace it.

The sensor bolts on to a flange, so there is no problem with refitting correctly. However, when doing this, watch out for any rust on the mating surface. Frank says it is amazing how little it takes to detrimentally affect the quality of the signal. Clean corrosion away carefully.

In some instances, where the output signal might be found to be poor but not actually faulty, it is possible to remove some of the plastic body of the sensor so that the

TECHNICAL SPECIFICATIONS

COMPONENT	OUTPUT
O$_2$ sensor	200/800 mV @ 1Hz or greater
Mass air flow meter	Idle 0.7V Cruise 1.3V Snap 3.7V
Injector duration	Cold 4ms Hot 2.6ms Cranking 12ms Snap 16-20ms Deceleration 1ms
Idle control valve	3-6V sawtooth signal
Vehicle speed sensor	Digital 12V to ground
Crank angle sensor	A/C 1¼ offset peak-to-peak 5V+ @ idle Cranking 2½
Camshaft position sensor	A/C peak-to-peak 8V @ idle
Coolant sensor (NTC)	Cold 3-4V Hot 0.5V
Ambient air sensor	15°C – 2.25-2.50V
Throttle position sensor	0.5V closed 4.5V open throttle

Using a break-out box linked to an oscilloscope is the only practical way for an independent specialist to tackle EEC V diagnostics.

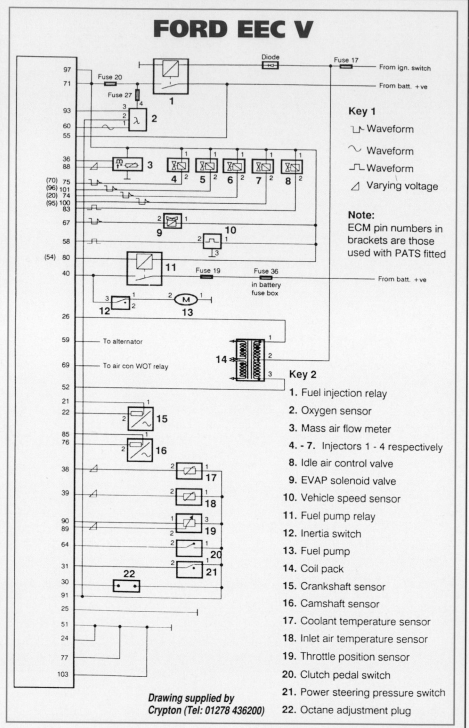

FORD EEC V

Key 1

⎍ Waveform
∿ Waveform
⊓⊔ Waveform
◁ Varying voltage

Note:
ECM pin numbers in brackets are those used with PATS fitted

Drawing supplied by
Crypton (Tel: 01278 436200)

Key 2

1. Fuel injection relay
2. Oxygen sensor
3. Mass air flow meter
4. - 7. Injectors 1 - 4 respectively
8. Idle air control valve
9. EVAP solenoid valve
10. Vehicle speed sensor
11. Fuel pump relay
12. Inertia switch
13. Fuel pump
14. Coil pack
15. Crankshaft sensor
16. Camshaft sensor
17. Coolant temperature sensor
18. Inlet air temperature sensor
19. Throttle position sensor
20. Clutch pedal switch
21. Power steering pressure switch
22. Octane adjustment plug

---

probe is actually moved slightly nearer to the flywheel, to boost the signal strength. Half a millimetre will make a significant difference, so take great care if you opt for this approach. Once again, this type of operation must be performed in conjunction with an oscilloscope, because this is the only way the signal can be meaningfully assessed.

Sometimes this type of adjustment can benefit a car's starting performance under 'hard start' conditions – cold weather, low cranking speed etc. But it should not be regarded as the complete solution. Problems with the battery, starter motor or sensor condition should ideally be corrected first. Remember that the quality of this signal output is determined by cranking

speed, the width of the air gap between sensor and flywheel, and the strength of the sensor's magnet. Variation in any of these will have a direct effect. Magnetism can be lost through the block and, in these cases, this type of modification can be a possible solution.

Finally, unless servicing is carried out to a good and thorough standard with this type of modern multi-valve engine, particularly with regard to oil changes, there will almost certainly eventually be problems with sticking valves and/or tappets. This can be caused either by lacquer deposits from the fuel causing the valves to grip momentarily in their guides, at which point the tappet takes the gap up and then prevents the valve from seating completely, or because of contami-

nants in the oil causing the tappets to continue to be pumped open.

Service intervals on modern cars are getting ever longer and, while quality lubricants and spark plugs can cope with this, these extended intervals do not take into account age-related problems or low use-type conditions. For example, 'shopping' cars could well go more than two years between services if the only criteria is mileage covered. So, clearly, under these conditions, problems may arise. Service on a six-monthly basis if usage levels are low is always the safest policy to ensure longevity.

NEXT MONTH
Vauxhall 2.5 V6

ELECTRONIC DIAGNOSTICS!

Tracing and fixing faults in electronic engine management systems

Number 44: *Vauxhall's gutsy 2.5-litre V6 can be found in Cavalier, Calibra, Omega and Vectra models, plus some Saabs. Chris Graham considers where problems can strike.*

This smooth Vauxhall V6 2.5-litre engine, which started life in top-of-the-range Cavaliers and Calibras and can now be found in Vectra and Omega models, is managed, in this latest form, by a Bosch Motronic system designated M2.8.3.

It provides total engine management, operating sequentially-controlled fuel injectors. There is closed

POSSIBLE PROBLEMS
1. **Bad earths**
2. **Software glitches**
3. **Alarm codes**

loop emission control and a few other interesting features, including secondary air induction. This version of the system arrived in 1994 but of course the engine was also fitted to Cavalier

and Calibra models before this.

The majority of the information detailed here will apply across the Vauxhall 2.5-litre V6 range, although slight differences should be expected relating to alarm systems, power steering and automatic gearboxes between the models. The same engine is used in some Saab models too, so they have a relevance here as well.

This Motronic version is not partic-

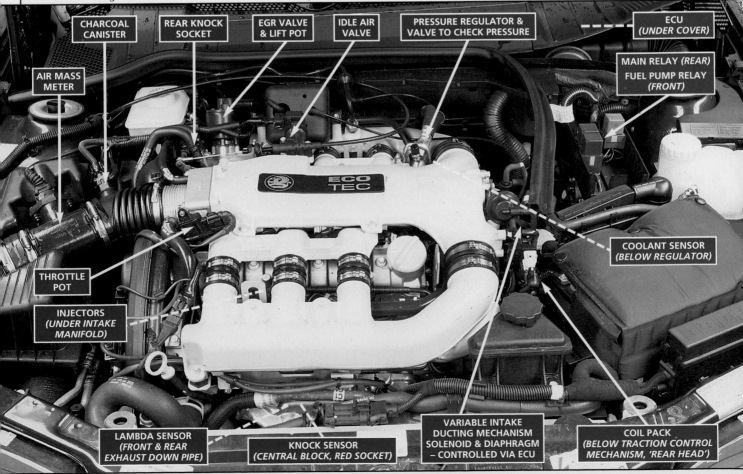

CHARCOAL CANISTER

REAR KNOCK SOCKET

EGR VALVE & LIFT POT

IDLE AIR VALVE

PRESSURE REGULATOR & VALVE TO CHECK PRESSURE

ECU (UNDER COVER)

AIR MASS METER

MAIN RELAY (REAR) FUEL PUMP RELAY (FRONT)

COOLANT SENSOR (BELOW REGULATOR)

THROTTLE POT

INJECTORS (UNDER INTAKE MANIFOLD)

LAMBDA SENSOR (FRONT & REAR EXHAUST DOWN PIPE)

KNOCK SENSOR (CENTRAL BLOCK, RED SOCKET)

VARIABLE INTAKE DUCTING MECHANISM SOLENOID & DIAPHRAGM – CONTROLLED VIA ECU

COIL PACK (BELOW TRACTION CONTROL MECHANISM, 'REAR HEAD')

ENGINE MANAGEMENT

The choice of components used in this system is relatively straightforward. However, Frank did note that on this particular Vectra there was an abundance of ECUs! Apart from the main engine management unit, there was one to control the traction, one for the encryption alarm system, and one for the power steering. If automatic transmission had been fitted, there would have been another for this too. Quite apart from the complexity of this arrangement, Frank believes there is a significant potential for age-related problems — impact damage, water ingress, corrosion and so on. What's more, these ECUs are all inter-linked, and tracking down a fault's cause could be a nightmare. The number of potential problems which could arise from the transmission of incorrect data between these ECUs is a worry too.

However, as far as the main components are concerned, there should be little to surprise you. You will find a thick film meter for measuring air intake, a bypass-type idle speed control valve, a coolant sensor, an ambient air temperature sensor, six standard fuel injectors, two Lambda sensors — one for each cylinder bank, a pair of knock control sensors and an EGR (exhaust gas recirculation) valve with lift potentiometer.

Additionally, there's a crank angle sensor, a camshaft phase sensor, a throttle position indicator, relays for powering up the ECU and for the fuel pump, an in-tank fuel pump, a powerful secondary air pump (to promote efficient Lambda sensor switching during engine warm up) with its own control relay, a charcoal canister for dealing with tank emissions and a DIS ignition system with triple coil pack.

The traction control system works in a combined way. Not only does the detection of wheel spin (via the ABS sensors) cause injectors to be switched off, but it also triggers gates in the induction system to effectively reduce engine torque.

The ECU is on the bulkhead on the nearside of the vehicle. It's reached from under the bonnet, by removing a sequence of plastic and metal covers. Frank's concern about this location relates to water ingress. If the covers aren't replaced correctly, water will run off the screen and straight down into the ECU compartment.

The ECU's size varies, depending on vehicle type and system version. The latest cars are fitted with an 88-pin unit, as per our diagram here, while the earlier applications feature a more standard 55-pin unit.

The system is code-readable, via the J1962 socket located under a trim panel just ahead of the handbrake lever. The problem, of course, can be finding a code reader which will be capable of handling this modern system. Sykes-Pickavant have yet to release a software pod for this recent application, but we're told that one is not far away.

When this arrives it will bring with it the possibility of retrieving stored fault codes, clearing them, driving actuators (injectors, coils, EGR valve etc) and obtaining live data. On the more recent software versions, the level of data available is both impressive and valuable.

---

ularly DIY-friendly. According to Frank Massey, proprietor of Preston-based Fuel Injection Services (Tel: 01772 201597), getting to grips with it involves the use of relatively sophisticated diagnostic techniques, both in terms of the initial approach and the ultimate repair.

As far as the Vectra pictured here is concerned, one potential problem under the bonnet is over-crowding. Some components are somewhat tucked away, although it should be added that, generally, the designers have done well in ensuring that most are reasonably accessible.

From a service point of view, tasks such as timing belt replacement have become an important issue. Not only is the belt long, but it runs within a split plastic cover with a sealing rubber. Failure to ensure that this rubber is correctly seated can cause it to foul the belt, resulting in it jumping.

PREPARATION

There are no major concerns to report with regard to this V6 application. Plugs obviously need to be removed and checked, and care is needed to avoid damaging the ceramic lead inserts. Frank suspects that, in common with many applications nowadays, these leads can only be bought in sets, so a careless breakage can represent an expensive mistake. On Vectra applications access is limited by the induction manifolds, which need to be removed first.

The idle control valve is simplicity itself on the Vectra, being located prominently on top of the engine at the back. We've not mentioned the prospect of cleaning the EGR valve so far in this series. Because these units are dealing with exhaust gases containing hard based carbon, they can stick, preventing them from closing fully. On the Vectra the valve is fitted with a lift potentiometer to detect just such a problem and the unit is sensed so that a fault code is generated should the fault arise.

The EGR valve must be cleaned ultrasonically — this is the only way to remove the hard and brittle deposits. Frank also believes that the valve should be changed on cars which have covered more than 40,000 miles, together with components such as the Lambda sensors.

These latest spec. Motronic systems are more sensitive to changes in performance of the Lambda sensors, so deterioration in performance is going to be more noticeable. There is a block learn capability, of course, but Frank thinks that, even so, replacement

should be seriously considered to keep engine performance in peak condition.

The air induction system isn't especially prone to clogging or suffering with contamination on this engine but,

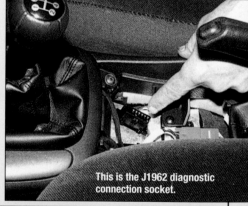

This is the J1962 diagnostic connection socket.

The orange-coloured plastic device around the HT lead in the centre of this picture is a clever little 'grabber' which Vauxhall provide for assisting with the removal of the plug leads.

ELECTRONIC DIAGNOSTICS!

nevertheless, a few squirts with carburettor cleaner can do nothing but good. The same applies to the main throttle body.

FAULT FINDING

Traditionally Frank says that, across the range, Vauxhalls have tended to suffer more than their fair share of wiring-related problems. These often relate to a tightness in the loom resulting from insufficient slack in the wiring. Components and connections are stressed, so faults inevitably arise as the years pass.

However, not all the problems take a long while to appear.

Frank has heard that, already, some earthing defects have been experienced on the Vectra. The root of the trouble appears to be the main earth points for the instrumentation and the engine management system, which are both to be found close to the ECU, up above the passenger footwell.

If resistance on these two becomes high then there are serious knock-on effects. Frank has been told that the crankshaft speed and position sensor signal is defeated – whether by the alarm system or the poor earth directly, he is not sure. One other strange quirk of the condition is that the indicators flash. Frank presumes this is caused by a knock-on problem with the relevant relay.

These earth points are accessed from within the passenger compartment, not under the bonnet as with the ECU itself. Remember that, with this modern application, as with most others today, the earth references are critical. It is not a matter of just measuring pure voltage. Tests cannot be made statically. Current flow is needed so that the voltage drop can be noted, but remember that this may only be for the period when the current is flowing.

Fast switching causes practical problems unless you have high quality diagnostic equipment — the voltage drops may be taking place in just a few milliseconds. A multimeter will simply not be able to pick up such subtleties. An oscilloscope provides the only solution if you want to prove a poor earth.

Frank adds that, as a matter of course now, he never repairs a

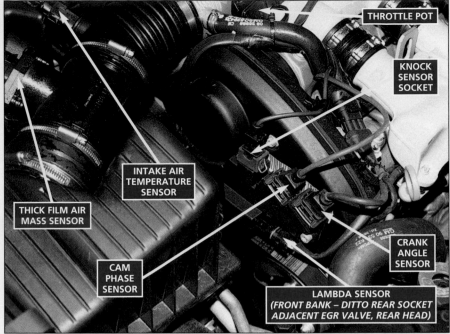

THROTTLE POT

KNOCK SENSOR SOCKET

INTAKE AIR TEMPERATURE SENSOR

THICK FILM AIR MASS SENSOR

CAM PHASE SENSOR

CRANK ANGLE SENSOR

LAMBDA SENSOR
(FRONT BANK – DITTO REAR SOCKET ADJACENT EGR VALVE, REAR HEAD)

poor earth as a solution but prefers to directly wire it back to the battery as a more suitable and lasting answer. He would recommend this approach in this case too.

The good news for owners of the most recent version of Motronic 2.8 is that the ECU is programmable. This means that any software changes introduced by Vauxhall can be programmed into your car without the need to physically change the ECU. This is achieved by the main dealer, via the J1962 socket in the car, and is a simple operation.

Having said this, this facility is something of a double-edged sword. The fact that such regular updates are available rather implies a need for them, if you see what I mean! Frank has heard that there are a number of 'spurious' faults which do occur, certainly on Vectra models, which appear to relate to little more than glitches within the software. Frank has heard that there are a number of 'spurious' faults which do occur, certainly on Vectra models, which appear to relate to little more than glitches within the software.

Just a few examples of these are as follows. A flagged fault with the air mass flow sensor (coded PO100) is one. Others are highlighted problems with the power steering, the same for the knock sensor (PO325) and one for the air conditioning relay (P1530). All of these will trigger the dashboard engine management warning light and will require a trip to the main dealer for this to be corrected.

In each case, there's no actual fault to worry about, but because all you have to go on is the 'anonymous' warning lamp, no chances can be taken and the problem must be investigated.

Continuing on the same theme, there is another point worth highlighting, which relates to the vehicle alarm. The latest Vectra operates a two-part digital security

TECHNICAL SPECIFICATIONS

ECU PIN	COMPONENT	VALUE
2/29	Idle control valve	12V, duty controlled
61	Carbon solenoid	12V to ground, duty/frequency controlled
19	Oxygen sensor	0.2-0.8V @ 1Hz+
20/78	Crank angle sensor	NOT AVAILABLE
17	Air mass meter	Static 0V Idle 0.73V 2K 1.14V 3K 1.46V WoT 4.5V linear
38	Camshaft ID	NOT AVAILABLE
7/35	Induction control solenoid	12V to ground
40/70	Knock sensor	Active 1-3V A/C
16	Air temp. sensor	3.45V @ 22°C
15	EGR valve (inc lift pot)	Closed 0.78V Open 4.0V
66		12V to ground
63	Pump relay	Off 12V On 0.5V
37	Secondary air relay	Off 12V On 0.5V
79	Vehicle speed sensor	NOT AVAILABLE
74	NTC coolant sensor	Cold 3.5V Hot 1.0V
N/A	Power steering	Input to ECU Idle 0.6V In motion 1.75V
	Injectors	
3	Cyl. 1	
31	Cyl. 2	Sequential injection with modified duration
4	Cyl. 3	Cold 4ms
31	Cyl. 4	Hot 2.5ms
5	Cyl. 5	Snap 14ms
33	Cyl. 6	

23

This is where you will find the ECU on the Vectra, tucked away beneath this flexible plastic panel, and two further bolted ones below.

code system. The key and the alarm ECU interact, compare notes and, if there is a problem, the vehicle will not be allowed to start.

If the key being used is the wrong one, or the code is not recognised for some other reason, the situation will be 'flagged' by the engine management light on the dash which will flash rapidly. This action should not be confused with an engine management fault.

As far as security code encryption is concerned, this is another dealer-only job. Once again this is achieved through the J1962 socket using Vauxhall's in-house diagnostics hardware, Tech 2. Up to five keys can be encrypted for one car and none is a master. The biggest problem you are likely to have is if you buy a car without its original 'code card', which details the security numbering relating specifically to the vehicle. Applying to Vauxhall for duplicates can take time, as definite proof of ownership is required.

NEXT MONTH
Audi A4.

BOSCH MOTRONIC M2.8.3

Diagram supplied by Equiptech from CAPS, the PC-based fuel injection manual. Tel: 01703 862240. Drawn by Martin White.

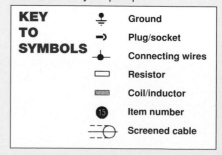

Vehicle speed sensor
Fuel injection warning light
Automatic transmission
Tachometer
Air conditioning

KEY

1. Electronic control unit
2. Ignition coil
4. Fuel injector
5. Idle speed control valve
6. Carbon filter solenoid valve
7. Fuel injection relay
8. Fuel pump
9. Oxygen sensor
10. Crankshaft position sensor
13. Coolant temperature sensor
15. Diagnostic socket
16. Spark plugs
17. Fuel pump fuse
18. Throttle potentiometer
20. Induction switchover solenoid valve
21. Knock sensor
22. Air flow meter (hotwire/film type)
23. Air temperature sensor
24. Exhaust gas recirculation control solenoid
25. Fuel pump relay
30. Camshaft sensor
31. Secondary air fuse
32. Secondary air relay
33. Secondary air switchover valve
34. Secondary air pump

KEY TO SYMBOLS		
⏚		Ground
→)		Plug/socket
•—		Connecting wires
▭		Resistor
▨		Coil/inductor
⑮		Item number
⊏⊃—		Screened cable

ELECTRONIC DIAGNOSTICS!

Tracing and fixing faults in electronic engine management systems

Number 45: *Chris Graham investigates the intricacies of Volkswagen's state-of-the-art Simos engine management system.*

The Simos total engine management package arrived in August 1994 and is found on a number of VW models including two-litre versions of the Golf, Corrado, Passat, Vento and the new Sharan MPV.

Frank Massey, our resident diagnostic expert and proprietor of Preston-based Fuel Injection Services (Tel: 01772 201597), is generally im-

POSSIBLE PROBLEMS
1. **Lambda sensor**
2. **Engine stalling**
3. **Rich mixture**

pressed with the system. While he admits that it does have a few characteristic failings, none is terribly serious and he compliments the general layout

and overall component quality.

Most things under the bonnet are easy to access and wiring runs are generally short. The Simos system took over from the ageing, but essentially reliable, Digifant management package and the most obvious 'give-away' between the two is that specification has switched from an air flow to an air mass meter on the later system.

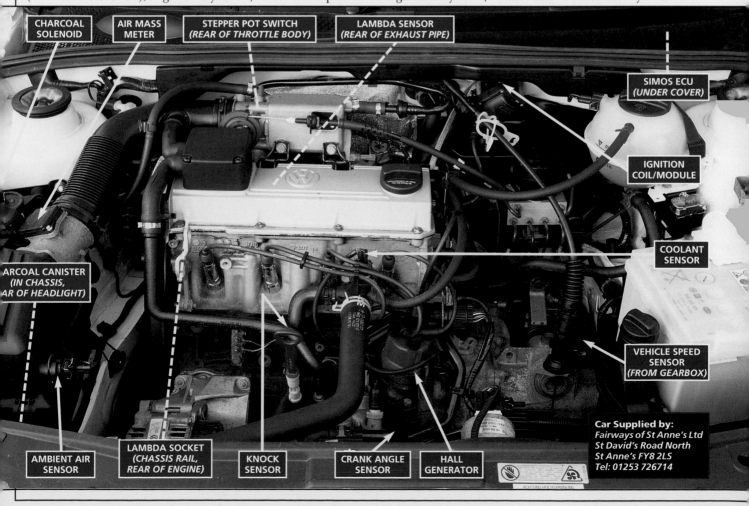

CHARCOAL SOLENOID

AIR MASS METER

STEPPER POT SWITCH *(REAR OF THROTTLE BODY)*

LAMBDA SENSOR *(REAR OF EXHAUST PIPE)*

SIMOS ECU *(UNDER COVER)*

IGNITION COIL/MODULE

COOLANT SENSOR

VEHICLE SPEED SENSOR *(FROM GEARBOX)*

ARCOAL CANISTER *(IN CHASSIS, AR OF HEADLIGHT)*

AMBIENT AIR SENSOR

LAMBDA SOCKET *(CHASSIS RAIL, REAR OF ENGINE)*

KNOCK SENSOR

CRANK ANGLE SENSOR

HALL GENERATOR

ENGINE MANAGEMENT

The entire Simos system is managed by a single 68-pin ECU which is found under a plastic cover immediately in front of the bulkhead, on the nearside of the vehicle – close to the pollen filter.

It operates multipoint fuel injection with sequentially controlled injectors. The ignition system is very 'traditional' with a distributor cap, rotor arm and five leads. There is an external ignition module/amplifier unit, although the trigger for this is supplied directly from the ECU. This is built into the back of the coil pack and, to date, Frank has never seen a failure.

Other major components of note include: a crank angle sensor which is mounted at the back of the block and generates a square wave signal; a Hall effect signal generator found inside the distributor – used to control the timing of the injectors accurately; a coolant sensor mounted next to the thermostat housing; an ambient air temperature sensor; an air mass meter, within the main air trunking into the engine; a pressure regulator within the standard fuel rail; a knock sensor at the front of the block with a screened lead

running directly back to the ECU; a vehicle speed sensor mounted in the gearbox, producing a digital signal indicating vehicle movement; a carbon canister control solenoid; a four-wire (with two separate earths) Lambda sensor mounted conventionally in the exhaust downpipe at the rear of the engine; an idle control system which incorporates a totally enclosed stepper motor together with a throttle potentiometer and an idle contact switch. This is all built into the throttle body assembly and not available separately.

Engine idle is digitally controlled. The device is spring-loaded, with one side permanently live and the other side ECU ground driven. By pulsing the motor the gear-operated plunger is adjusted to regulate idle speed. When the pulse is removed, the spring loading retracts the plunger via a mechanical action.

The relays are located in the main fuse box inside the car, just above the driver's right knee position. There is a J1962 diagnostic socket located conveniently behind a small trim panel on the dashboard, just above the cigarette lighter. A full set of fault

codes is provided but these can only be accessed using a hand-held reader. There appears to be no way of displaying them in 'blink code' form.

Frank was unable to be specific about which of the independently-made code readers could be used on this system. Volkswagen obviously have their own diagnostic equipment for dealer-only use. There is, of course, a full 'limp home' mode offered should an important component fail, and a 'block learn' capability as well. The latter can be cleared by removing the ECU's power supply, reconnecting it and then driving the car for about 10 minutes under varying road conditions.

Note that, on this engine application, it is still possible to rotate the distributor but, because the actual timing signal is not generated by this component any more, all that will happen is that the phase signal will be upset. This will affect injector timing and so possibly upset combustion efficiency. The best advice is to leave this well alone! The fuel pump is located within the tank in the conventional manner.

PREPARATION

Something which is always well worth checking on these VW 2.0-litre Simos applications is the distributor cap. Internal soiling and contamination is relatively common and must be dealt with as part of your basic preparation procedure. In addition, the cap is covered by a black plastic shroud which can, in fact, do more harm than good. In the worst cases it can actually mask the build up of contamination on the cap itself.

The distributor is positioned at the front of the engine, and mounted low down, so it is rather vulnerable to road grime and moisture. Frank's advice is always to remove the plastic shield and then the cap as well. Clean and dry both thoroughly. You are very likely to find signs of electrical tracking in the cap. It does no harm to dispose of the plastic cover altogether if you so choose.

Often you will find the rotor arm to be in a bad state, particularly the resistor section in the centre of the arm. If you have any doubts about this then replace it with a new one. With regard to spark plugs, Volkswagen are one of the manufacturers who now specify multiple electrode plugs. The only purpose of this choice, Frank says, is to maximise plug service life. He does not believe that these components offer any improvement in spark quality and so sees little practical point in their use.

He is a firm believer in the idea that conventional, single-electrode plugs, of the right heat range, type and electrode length, are perfectly adequate for the job. Top quality platinum plugs, from NGK for example, will normally last significantly longer (40-60,000 miles) than a triple-electrode plug and are usually more affordable too. Need we say more?

Original equipment lead quality is pretty good according to Frank, apart from a potential weakness at the plug end. He says they feature a metal shroud which actually extends down to cover the plug. This is intended to act as an RF barrier and also as a heat shield, both of which it does. The problem, however, is that if sufficient contamination builds up within this shroud

then its metal construction will actively promote electrical tracking and plug spark efficiency will be lost.

As a matter of course, Frank's remedy for this is to cut off the metal shrouds, once they have become aged and discoloured, and to replace them with the latest generation rubberised version from BMW. He considers these a superior product and adds that

The crank angle sensor is tucked away down here, below the distributor.

ELECTRONIC DIAGNOSTICS!

they are easily fitted assuming the correct crimping tool is used. Fitting kits are available from dealers.

The air intake system will rarely provide any problems but it is well worth checking anyway. Contamination is unlikely on this 2.0-litre engine. The stepper motor is completely remote from the throttle body so there should be few problems here either.

Apart from this, just cast an eye generally over the engine looking for obvious signs of air leaks from vacuum hoses etc. Note also that the main air intake is a semi-rigid plastic construction which can be damaged by careless handling. It is secured with 'aggressive' spring clips which have to be released using pliers. If these are not removed from the hose after disconnection, the spring-loading will crush the pipe, possibly leading to fracturing and needless extra expense.

TACKLING TROUBLE

The first and probably the most common problem associated with this Volkswagen engine/management package is water ingress into the Lambda sensor socket. The classic symptoms will be a car which is running 'roughly' and probably rich as well. The management system will have been thrown into 'default' because Lambda switching will be out of specification or non-existent.

The positioning of this sensor socket, low down at the back of the engine, causes all the problems. Frank believes it to be located directly below the water drainage point from the back of the bulkhead.

The sensor itself is very sensitive to water ingress so problems are all but assured! On a number of occasions Frank has been forced to cut out badly corroded sockets because they have been rusted solid. One example he saw recently was running extremely rich. An emissions checked showed the HC level to be 9% at the tailpipe which, for a catalyst-equipped car, was worrying! Upon inspection it was found that the sensor wires had rotted away completely within the socket. The sensor had to be replaced and the wiring repaired, after which the engine returned to normal running.

Few problems should be caused by the idle control mechanism on this VW application.

Frank's advice, however, is not simply to change the sensor itself and leave it at that. You must be sure that there are no other associated or contributory factors. Certainly, in most cases, switching the sensor will put the car right, but don't forget the basics. Make sure that the spark plugs are good and that all the other main inputs to the ECU are correct.

To check the switching action of the Lambda sensor effectively you really must use an oscilloscope. The sensor switches between 0.2-0.8V at 1Hz+ and so its earth reference must be exceptionally good. If this switching is correct then the engine is certainly fuelling is as it should. If not, there is a fuelling problem elsewhere. It could be a simple air leak-related problem or one caused by a blocked or faulty injector. Incorrect fuel pressure can be another source of trouble.

Remember also that fuelling problems in themselves can lead to Lambda sensor failure. Once the component

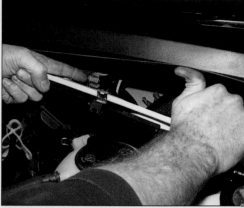

ECU is located beneath this flexible plastic cover at the rear of the engine bay.

becomes coated with soot, its sensitivity will be adversely affected. There is no way to effectively clean a dirty Lambda sensor, not even by using ultrasonic equipment, so a replacement is the only solution.

Another relatively common problem on these vehicles relates to actual engine stalling. This occurs most commonly when the engine is hot, but can happen at any other time as well. The cause is normally a straightforward one, and is that the intermittent pulse signal to the stepper motor from the ECU is lost.

With the most recent occurrence of this, Frank found that the stepper had a 12V supply in and out, meaning that, in effect, there was no ground signal. Under normal conditions this should be provided by the ECU in response to an engine speed signal.

If you discover this problem, the motor's operation should be tested manually. Carefully remove the throttle body and take great care to make sure that the wiring codes are right. There are six wires running into the connector socket. Only two of them go to the motor, one being

TECHNICAL SPECIFICATIONS

ECU pin	Component	Value
40	Throttle pot	4.2V closed, 0.8V open
18	Idle contact	0V closed, 12V open
41	Throttle pos ind	5V supply
25	Idle motor	12V (white wire)
30		Pulsed to ground (black wire)
67-68	Engine speed sensor	12V digital
16		Screen
44	Hall (distributor)	12v digital
7	Amp trigger	1.2V digital
12	Coolant temp sensor	2.5V cold, 0.3V hot
2	Injector 1	Durations are 4ms hot
46	Injector 2	16+ms hot snap,
47	Injector 3	10ms hot crank
48	Injector 4	Saturated pulse
34/36	Knock sensor	1-2V A/C
29	Air temp sensor	3V @ 20°C
33	Charcoal solenoid	0V on (open)
31	Fuel pump relay	0V on
17	Lambda sensor	0.2-0.8V @ 1Hz+
8	Main relay	0V on

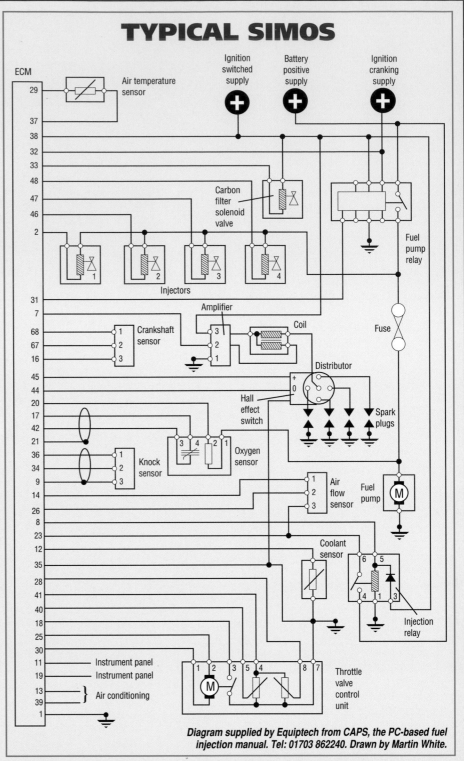

TYPICAL SIMOS

Diagram supplied by Equiptech from CAPS, the PC-based fuel
injection manual. Tel: 01703 862240. Drawn by Martin White.

a supply wire and the other the pulse ground wire. By connecting this to a 12V battery supply you can index the motor to check its operation. The instant you connect up you should hear the motor being driven and then, following disconnection, you will notice the return spring resetting the unit.

Problems with the motor itself are rare, says Frank, so unfortunately trouble of this sort normally points to an ECU failure. However, before condemning the 'brain', make quite sure that there is continuity between it and the stepper motor.

The third, relatively common failing with this application, relates to fuelling. Often it will not be highlighted until the vehicle fails the MoT test. These modern systems switch into 'limp home' mode so smoothly, and the driveability under these 'default' conditions remains so good, that most owners are completely unaware that anything is wrong! Even fuel consumption remains acceptable.

Nevertheless, the mixture will be sufficiently rich to show up at testing time and a common cause of this is a problem with the coolant sensor. This is a composite component, meaning that it is actually two units in one. One half provides the coolant value voltage to the ECU, in response to water temperature, while the other half controls the thermal coupling device for the electric cooling fan.

These sensors are prone to failure and when this happens they default into open circuit. The ECU 'sees' a reference voltage only (of 5V) instead of a normal output value and the result is that the engine begins to over-fuel, once the ECU has switched into limp home mode. Fortunately, replace-

ments are easily fitted and very affordable – costing about £10.

There are likely to be some knock-on effects of this too. As we mentioned earlier, the Lambda sensor can be badly affected. So if this type of problem is isolated, it will be worth checking the operation of the Lambda as well. There may well also be question marks over the catalyst. Frank's advice is to allow the car to be used normally for a month or so, which will give the cat time to recover by cleaning itself up, if it is still capable of doing so.

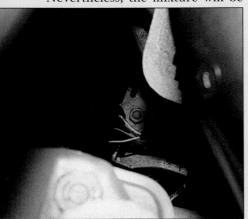

The four-wire Lambda sensor is rather more awkward to get at, being mounted low down at the rear of the engine.

NEXT MONTH
ROVER 600

Lucas  TEST EQUIPMENT

LASER 2000

... will find the faults in cars yet to be designed.

The electronic systems in today's vehicles are becoming more and more sophisticated. They control many aspects of performance from fuelling and braking, through to driver information.

The success of any workshop is increasingly dependent on its ability to diagnose and repair these systems. Many vehicles now incorporate a dedicated diagnostic link or serial port to enable quick and accurate testing.

The serial port tester is a result of these developments. Designed and manufactured using the experience gained in developing vehicle electronic systems, as well as diagnostics for vehicle manufacturers.

Features and benefits.

The **Laser 2000** incorporates a unique plug-in hardware module and specific plug-in software modules that provide the flexibility for the tester to evolve with the ever changing systems and standards for vehicle electronic systems. The engineers in Lucas responsible for designing engine systems for decades into the future, use Laser 2000 in the development of the diagnostics for those systems. This is possible because even the most significant changes to future system designs can be simply catered for with the provision of a new plug-in hardware module.

The operator simply installs the appropriate module, and then connects the **Laser 2000** to the vehicle's diagnostic serial port using the appropriate adaptor cable.

In carrying out many of the tests, **Laser 2000** is not restricted to the workshop. Once connected, the vehicle may be taken out for a full road test, enabling detection of even the most elusive intermittent faults. Faults identified during road tests may be stored in the memory for investigation back in the workshop.

BRAKE FLUID TESTER

Over a period of time all brake fluid absorbs moisture from the atmosphere. This reduces the boiling point of the fluid which increase the risk of brake failure during heavy braking.

The **Lucas Brake Tester** allows you to check the boiling point of brake fluid to determine how much moisture has been absorbed, giving an accurate warning of when the fluid needs to be changed.

The new **Lucas Brake Fluid Tester** YWB211 offers many advantages over other brake fluid testers.

PORTABLE OSCILLOSCOPE

Comes with one less feature than the expensive kind...the expense.

The Oscilloscope has become an essential piece of service equipment in today's modern garage.

The **Lucas Oscilloscope** is a fully portable tester with an impressive features list. It can be used in conjunction with other test equipment found in the workshop, including multimeters and clampmeters. The extensive level of functionality incorporated into the Oscilloscope also means that it can replace the need for several other testers, and reduce the cost of building a powerful diagnostics kit.

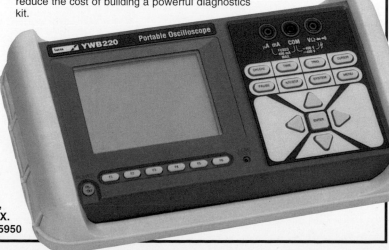

FOR MORE INFORMATION CONTACT:
Test Equipment,
Lucas Aftermarket Operations,
Stratford Road, Solihull, B90 4AX.
Tel: 0121 506 5955 Fax: 0121 506 5950

ic Now we offer the largest range of exchange ECUs and Airflow Meters in the UK.

Not only do Webcon have the ultimate range, but also the in-depth technical expertise to back it up. For virtually every make of car.

We can deliver our exchange ECUs and airflow meters overnight. Orders received before 5pm will be delivered a.m. the next day. Own unit repairs are handled and returned within 24 hours. Alternatively we have more than 300 outlets who in many cases can supply you from stock.

This typifies the total Webcon offer...the most comprehensive range of service components for all kinds of fuel systems. And that includes injectors, carburettors, air filters, fuel pumps, turbo-chargers and associated parts.

For further details, contact the Sales Department on 01932 787100.

WEBCON

WEBCON U.K. LIMITED, Dolphin Road, Sunbury-on-Thames, Middlesex TW16 7HE. Fax: 01932 782725.
E-mail: sales@webcon.co.uk Web-site on: http://www.webcon.co.uk

ELECTRONIC DIAGNOSTICS!

Tracing and fixing faults in electronic engine management systems

Number 46: Chris Graham digs beneath the bonnet of Rover's smart 600 in search of electronic gremlins, niggles and other annoyances.

The smartly-styled Rover 600 is available with a number of different engine configurations. The car featured here is a late 620 version with complete engine management provided by the Rover PGM-FI (Programmed Multipoint Fuel Injection) system.

The 2-litre engine is not a new unit and still bears many similarities to the

---

POSSIBLE PROBLEMS
1. **MAP sensor pipe**
2. **EGR valve**
3. **Fast idle**

---

motor found under the bonnet of the Honda Accord. The ECU is located in the traditional place under a kick plate in the passenger footwell. One change is

that the control unit used to feature an LED for displaying fault codes – this no longer appears to be the case. These are now read via a light on the dashboard.

Frank Massey, proprietor of Fuel Injection Services (Tel: 01772 201597) believes this system to have a full serial communication capability, meaning that 'raw' data can be extracted via a J1962 socket.

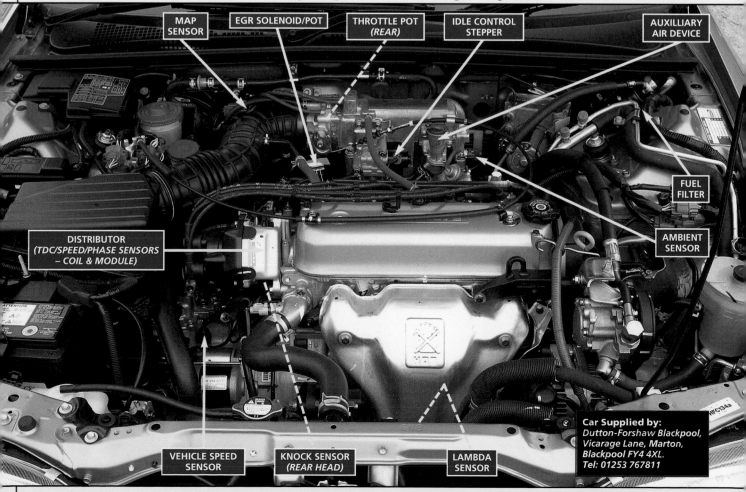

MAP SENSOR · EGR SOLENOID/POT · THROTTLE POT (REAR) · IDLE CONTROL STEPPER · AUXILLIARY AIR DEVICE · FUEL FILTER · AMBIENT SENSOR · DISTRIBUTOR (TDC/SPEED/PHASE SENSORS – COIL & MODULE) · VEHICLE SPEED SENSOR · KNOCK SENSOR (REAR HEAD) · LAMBDA SENSOR

Car Supplied by:
*Dutton-Forshaw Blackpool, Vicarage Lane, Marton, Blackpool FY4 4XL.
Tel: 01253 767811*

ENGINE MANAGEMENT

This version of PGM-FI provides multi-point fuel injection, with closed loop emissions control and exhaust gas recirculation (EGR). There is a traditional approach to engine ignition with a conventional, Lucas-made distributor. This contains three pick-ups which provide the key inputs for the ECU's control of the sequential fuel injectors.

These consist of a cylinder sensor to confirm camshaft position, a TDC sensor and a crankshaft sensor which is sometimes referred to as an engine speed sensor. There is also an internally mounted ignition module together with a coil.

Other significant components in the system include: an EGR solenoid which allows exhaust gases to be recirculated back into the intake; an EGR position sensor which is a potentiometer mounted on top of the EGR valve to determine its position; a purge valve to control hydrocarbon flow back into the manifold; a manifold pressure sensor (MAP); an air intake temperature sensor; a throttle position sensor; a coolant temperature sensor.

There is a choice of oxygen sensors – either two-wire or four-wire heated, and the latter was fitted in this case; also there was an inertia switch; a throttle potentiometer on the end of the throttle spindle; main relay which is a dual unit; road speed sensor in the gearbox; four traditional fuel injectors and a fuel pump conventionally located in the tank.

Interestingly there are normally three systems used to control engine idle on this PGM-FI application. These are a thermal valve which is a water-heated, wax capsule-based component, an electronically controlled stepper motor in the form of a rotary control valve, and a manual air bleed for basic adjustment. Frank saw only the first two of these on this car.

There are other inputs supplied to the ECU which relate to vehicle specification, such as compressor clutch relay input on auto-equipped cars. There is also an immobilisation input from the encryption alarm system supplied by the alarm's own ECU and other, more obscure features such as an air bypass solenoid for controlling variable intake track, and an engine mount control solenoid.

The whole system, Frank says, is probably the most reliable system currently on the market.

PREPARATION

Generally speaking, there is not a lot to worry about as far as preparation is concerned with this model. The plugs, despite being mounted reasonably deeply in the engine, usually remain relatively clean and the leads rarely cause problems – Frank has never had to change a set!

The distributor cap can suffer from slight contamination build-up within, but this is never usually a real problem. This is due primarily to the fact that the cap is allowed to 'breathe' via a pipe plumbed either into the intake manifold or to atmosphere.

Intake and vacuum hoses are robust so cause very few problems unless they have been damaged by careless handling etc. The throttle body usually remains exceptionally clean too.

If you wish to pick up a negative signal for the purposes of an engine kill test then you will have to make a fly lead for connection to the distributor cap at the coil negative terminal, and route it outside. Low tension can be monitored from external cables but this will not allow you to carry out engine kill or cranking balance tests.

Don't forget the basics, though. Examine and replace spark plugs. Check leads for damage and assess wiring generally for any obvious signs of trouble.

TACKLING TROUBLE

Obviously the car featured here is very new and Frank would not envisage many serious problems with it at all. Nevertheless, there are some important points to watch for.

The most critical pipe in the whole engine runs from the air intake manifold to the MAP sensor. This provides the input responsible for interpreting the intake pulse to the engine and converts this into a voltage change so that the ECU can calculate correct fuelling.

This pipe, remarkably, is routed to include a very tight bend immediately before it enters the MAP sensor on the o/s bulkhead. Although this is obviously a pre-shaped pipe, Frank foresees problems with kinking or distortion which will have the effect of distorting or 'dampening' the pressure pulse.

There is also a possibility that this pipe may well collect deposits of oil or fuel which could have the same effect. Any distortion of the air pulsing and the response of the MAP sensor to change will be limited, so fuelling response will be adversely affected. Flat spots will result, together with hesitation and general driveability problems.

In Frank's opinion the routing of this pipe should be changed. He would fit a new pipe running straight to the sensor, without the bend, to hopefully eliminate the risk of trouble altogether.

There can also be MAP sensor-related problems on this application but Frank admits that they are rare. They create over-fuelling conditions and driveability trouble typically. Check the integrity of the connecting pipe using a vacuum gauge. Any drop in engine vacuum, for whatever reason, will affect the MAP sensor. Defects in valve seat performance, cambelt timing, other air leaks will all cause problems. You should read about 22in of mercury and this is a crucial factor.

TECHNICAL SPECIFICATIONS

ECU pin	Component	Value
A21/A22	Ignition module	Pin 1, CB drive to coil Pin 2, Digital trigger from ECM, 0-12V
B13/14	TDC sensor	Peak-to-peak cranking 2+V Idle 12+V
B15/15	RPM sensor	Peak-to-peak cranking 2+V Idle 12+V
B11/122	CID sensor	Peak-to-peak cranking 2+V Idle 12+V
D15	Air temp sensor	Cold 3V, Hot 1V, normal 2.25V
D13	Coolant temp sensor	Cold 2.5V, hot 0.5V
D17	MAP sensor	Atmos 2.8V, 20in/Hg 0.7V
D11	Throt pos indic.	Closed 0.5V, open 4.5V linear
D14	Oxygen sensor	0.2-0.8V @ 1Hz+
A20	Charcoal solenoid	0-12V, duty variable
A9	Idle control valve	0-12V digital, duty variable
A1-A4	Injectors	3-4.5ms cold crank 2-2.5ms hot idle, sequential control via resistor pack
B10	Veh speed sensor	0-12V, digital in motion
D12	EGR valve	0.5-4V, linear variable output related to load and temp

Even on this brand new Rover 620 note how the vitally important pipe leading into the MAP sensor is kinked.

ELECTRONIC DIAGNOSTICS!

A second problem Frank has come across on a few occasions concerns the exhaust gas recirculation valve. This can suffer from a build-up of carbon deposits within its port which prevent it from closing completely. In the past this type of fault would have been undetectable, apart from the fact that the engine ran badly. The EGR gases are normally only added to the engine under certain conditions, and never at low engine speeds because they will reduce engine efficiency.

ECU is protected by this rigid metal kick panel in the passenger footwell.

Frank is pointing to the EGR lift potentiometer. Arrowed is the electrical idle control motor.

The basic purpose of the EGR system is to reduce the production of nitrogen oxides by lowering the combustion temperature. The introduction of 'inert' exhaust gas must be accurately controlled by the ECU which drives the solenoid valve with a pulsed action. The amount of lift is now monitored by a potentiometer on top of the valve, so problems caused by carbon deposits should be much easier to identify.

The solenoid valve can stick, resulting in poor idle and a lowered manifold vacuum, because there is effectively an exhaust leak directly into the

INJECTORS

eq34825   ECU

D22 D13   D15   D11 D20   D12   D21 D17 D19

y/gr, rd/y, gr/w, rd/blu, y/w, w/blk, gr/w, y/w, w, y/rd

CTS   ATS   TPS   EGR valve lift sensor   MAP

IGNITION

EQ34462

ECU   A23   A24

B11 B12 B14 B13 B16 B15 A21 A22   earth

or   W   blu/y

w/blu, or/blu, blu/gr, y/gr

distributor multiplug

TDC sensor   2   1   rpm sensor

distributor

CID sensor

amplifier

tachometer

ignition coil

supply from ignition switch : t15

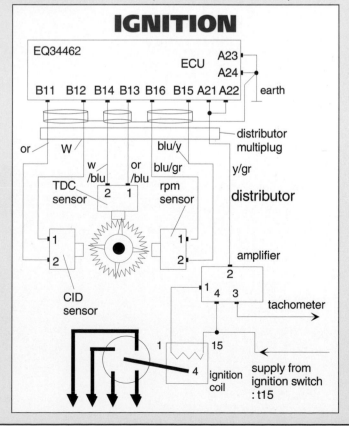

33

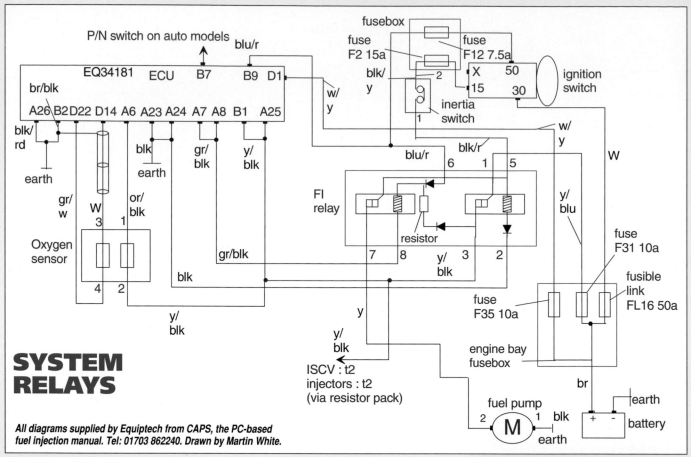

SYSTEM RELAYS

All diagrams supplied by Equiptech from CAPS, the PC-based fuel injection manual. Tel: 01703 862240. Drawn by Martin White.

manifold. Effective cleaning of the solenoid valve is difficult and Frank believes that replacement is the only practical solution. Ultrasonic cleaning provides the only possible option but even this will often prove ineffective.

Remember, also, that both these two potential faults will have a knock-on effect on the oxygen sensor. Problems here may well be flagged with an appropriate fault code, so be aware of the potential causes. Simply replacing the oxygen sensor may not provide the complete answer. Catalysts can suffer

PRIMARY SENSORS

supply from
FI relay : t3

from an over-fuelling problem too.

The third potential problem is highlighted by a fast engine idle. As we've already mentioned, idle is controlled by both electronic and mechanical means. The problem, in this case, lies with the mechanical side of things, and the wax-based capsule valve.

Essentially, this is a simple and reliable component. The wax is melted as water temperature rises and, under the influence of a strong spring, the valve is allowed to close. So when the engine is hot there should be no passage of air allowed. However, a couple of things can cause problems. One can be a straightforward defect within the cooling system of the engine.

If the thermostat has been removed or has failed in the 'open' position, the engine will run that much cooler, especially in cold weather. This will prevent the wax from being sufficiently heated to close the valve so idle speed will remain high. It is easy to assume this is an electrical problem and hours can be wasted in a futile search for the cause!

The other possibility might be a corrupted block learn system. Block learn, as we all should know by now, is the management system's ability to monitor sensors and adapt its output to changes in circumstances – compensating for wear etc. It can become corrupted for a number of reasons, according to Frank. On one occasion he had made all the normal checks for the cause of a fast idle and found everything to be in its correct

position. Only after disconnecting the negative battery terminal, to 'power down' the entire management system, then restarting the engine, did the problem resolve itself. A disconnection like this will 're-boot' the block learn, after which the car must be driven for 10-15 miles under varying conditions to re-establish all sensor outputs.

NEXT MONTH
TOYOTA CARINA E

ELECTRONIC DIAGNOSTICS!

Tracing and fixing faults in electronic engine management systems

Number 47: The Toyota Carina E goes under the electrical spotlight this month, as Chris Graham investigates its engine management system for bugs!

Toyota, in keeping with all other Japanese makes, enjoys a reputation for a high level of mechanical reliability. The cars simply go on and on and the Carina E is no exception. The model we are looking at here – the 1.6i – is a popular seller and while not a quick car, is a snappy performer too. In correct tune its engine is responsive, crisp and very

POSSIBLE PROBLEMS
1. **HT lead tracking**
2. **Lambda sensor**
3. **Injector problems**

well managed by Toyota's own TCCS system.

Frank Massey, proprietor of Preston-based Fuel Injection Services

(Tel: 01772 201597) and diagnostics training expert, was very impressed with the overall layout under the bonnet of this Toyota. He considers the general level of accessibility to be superb. Even though the engine itself is a relatively old design, he considers that it has been developed most effectively over the years and, as a consequence, is essentially reliable today.

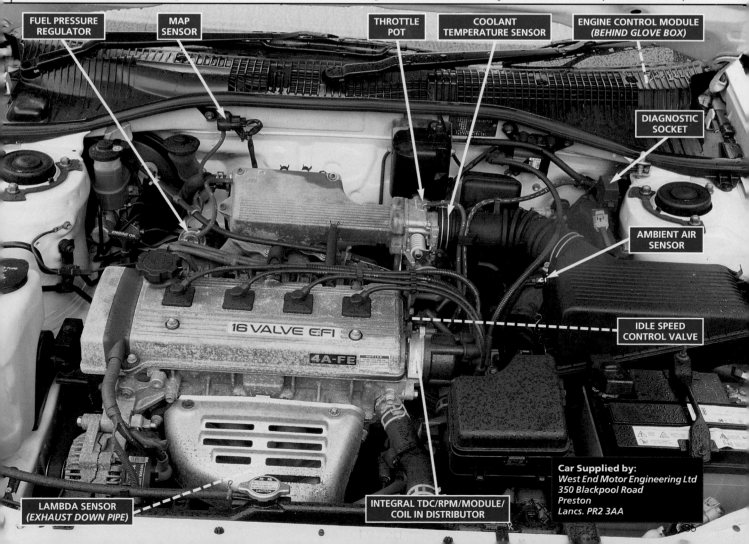

FUEL PRESSURE REGULATOR

MAP SENSOR

THROTTLE POT

COOLANT TEMPERATURE SENSOR

ENGINE CONTROL MODULE (BEHIND GLOVE BOX)

DIAGNOSTIC SOCKET

AMBIENT AIR SENSOR

IDLE SPEED CONTROL VALVE

16 VALVE EFI

4A-FE

LAMBDA SENSOR (EXHAUST DOWN PIPE)

INTEGRAL TDC/RPM/MODULE/ COIL IN DISTRIBUTOR

Car Supplied by:
West End Motor Engineering Ltd
350 Blackpool Road
Preston
Lancs. PR2 3AA

ENGINE MANAGEMENT

This 1.6-litre Toyota Carina E application employs a total engine management system referred to by Toyota as TCCS. It makes use of a reasonably traditional ignition system, consisting of a distributor cap with plug leads and a conventional coil. The system runs with intermittent, multipoint fuel injection so all four injectors are triggered by a common pulse. There is an in-tank fuel pump and a conventional fuel rail with a regulator at one end for controlling pressure.

The primary sensors and components included are as follows: a single relay for powering up the ECU; an open-circuit relay which is used to bring in the fuel pump when crank movement is sensed; a diode pack (in common with many Japanese vehicles) to ensure rapid response for injector switching; an externally-mounted MAP sensor; an ambient air temperature sensor found in the air induction system; an NTC engine coolant temperature sensor found at the rear of the head; a throttle position sensor which also incorporates an idle switch; a comprehensive diagnostic socket which can be used to interrogate various systems on the car. Blink codes are available and displayed by a warning light on the dashboard. This will warn the driver when problems have occurred, but will only reveal the relevant blink codes when two terminals in the data link connector socket – TE1 and E1 – are bridged. There are 26 listed fault codes, numbered variously from 11 to 78.

The system runs with closed-loop emissions control so there is a Lambda sensor and a catalytic converter. This sensor is a conventional Zirconium unit but utilises a flange-fitting, as opposed to the more common threaded approach.

The distributor is the key to the whole system. It contains the engine position and speed sensors, so there is no crank angle sensor on the front pulley to worry about. A trigger is sent from the distributor to the coil in the conventional way. In addition, there is an idle speed control valve which is driven by the ECU.

This engine used to rely on a totally independent ignition system with separate fuel control, but that combination has been ditched in favour of the total engine management package we see today.

PREPARATION

As with most other Japanese cars, you are not likely to find too much contamination in the air induction system on this Carina E. Nevertheless, remove the intake hose if you wish, and wash out the throttle body with carburettor cleaner and a brush. Problems are rare here but it is always worth checking just in case.

Take a peek inside the distributor cap, despite the fact that these don't normally suffer nearly as badly as European cars (Frank believes that the breather pipe has much to do with this). Wash it out and check the rotor arm carefully for signs of corrosion or erosion on the electrode. Caps will rarely have to be replaced.

The HT leads are of reasonable quality but at the spark plug end there can be problems. More of this later. Also make sure that the correct type and style of plug is fitted and that they are all correctly gapped. There are no other common problems to worry about with the wiring on this car.

Check the setting of the throttle stop. If you suspect that it has been fiddled with then run through the standard setting procedure to make sure it is right. Reset the stop so that the throttle disc shows just a couple of thou clearance from the body and then lock off the nut. If the system is telling you that there is a problem with the throttle position switch – the output value may be out of range – it could well be that either the stop has been incorrectly adjusted or that the potentiometer, which is adjustable, needs to be reset.

NEED TRAINING?
Frank Massey runs regular courses at his well-equipped Preston workshop; everything from basic engine management introductions to full-blown 'hands on', system-specific tuition. **Call 01772 201597 for details.**

The most vital hose on the car, from a management point of view, is the one running between the intake manifold and the MAP sensor. Check that there are no kinks or splits along its length.

TROUBLE-SHOOTING

The first and perhaps most common problem relates to the plug leads. These are of a modern design with, at the plug end, a rigid section which reaches down into the head and over the plug. This assembly can become electrically porous and so tracking is a risk. The leads are a tight fit within the head so any leaking spark simply passes into the head to produce a short or shunt.

This can be extremely difficult to find for several reasons. The voltage which is required to make the leap to the head can be very similar to that of the spark jumping across the standard plug electrode gap. Therefore, the problem can be masked. All looks normal. So check the condition and appearance of all plugs carefully as part of your preparation procedure. If there is any deviation away from the normal condition of the plug on any one out of the four plugs, then be suspicious that one may be tracking. If the leads look dirty, and usually they are not, wash and thoroughly dry them carefully.

Apart from checking the spark quality using an engine tuner or oscilloscope, Frank still likes to check each lead using the 'open circuit' method. While he admits that this technique is no longer recommended, he finds it most effective.

Simply disconnect one lead at a time at the plug end, while the engine is running. Allow the lead to rest across the top of the cam cover so that the spark cannot leap across to anything that is particularly sensitive, and notice what happens. If the spark can be seen jumping across to the engine top from anywhere other than the absolute end of the lead, then there is a problem.

Another typical problem on this Toyota application relates to a poor

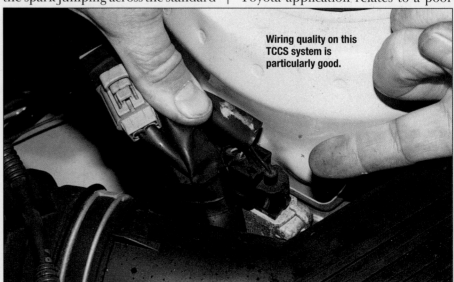

Wiring quality on this TCCS system is particularly good.

ELECTRONIC DIAGNOSTICS!

earthing on the Lambda sensor. We have already mentioned that this sensor has a flange-fitting into the exhaust downpipe. This means that it relies for its earth reference on the connection through the flange and this system has its inherent weaknesses.

When problems strike there is not a lot to be done apart from cleaning up the flange and, maybe, tapping out the threads. Most trouble like this will simply be flagged as a failed sensor, but before condemning the unit it is important to check the earth reference. When this becomes high the Lambda may still switch but the whole range of that switch will move up. Instead of switching from 0.2 to 0.8V, for example, it may be found to be switching between one and two volts, with an earth reference of one volt.

The consequence of this is that the ECU may well not recognise this switching action at all and could regard the whole thing as a signal to lean-off the mixture. The chances are that a new sensor will be required anyway and, at the replacement stage, Frank advises that the flange be filed off to a clean finish and the securing screw threads treated too.

Another option is to add a separate wire from one of the flange screws to the battery, to ensure a good earth. There is a problem with this, however. The wires used by the sensor are specially resistant to heat and most replacement, PVC-coated wire will not stand the harsh conditions of the environment.

There is also the possibility of fitting a different, non-original sensor. In theory Frank favours this approach and says that replacing the original with a four-wire component makes a lot of sense because an extra earth is provided for. However, he has heard rumours that this system is sensitive to the type of sensor fitted. He has been told of cases where non-original sensors have led to serious drivability problems on this application. For some reason the ECU cannot, or will not, recognise the new sensor.

In the past few months Frank has started to see, for the first time, a number of Japanese vehicles arriving in his workshop with fuel injector problems.

The excellent Advanced Code Reader from Sykes-Pickavant can be very usefully employed on this Toyota application.

Check plug lead boots for electrical tracking.

This is very out of character for these cars and Frank is currently putting the cause down to changes in fuel quality.

Such problems, caused by lacquer contamination, lead directly to noticeable drivability problems. The all-important spray pattern becomes affected and delivery rates deteriorate too. Because the fuel control on this and other Japanese engines is very tightly regulated, even a slight deviation away from the ideal causes a major problem.

The engine management system, although it has the ability to adapt its performance to changing conditions to some extent, cannot cope with poor fuelling quality. The only solution is to remove and thoroughly clean the injectors to reinstate their original performance levels. Frank says he has also noticed that the ultrasonic cleaning process he uses is taking longer to complete the job.

These sorts of problem are all inter-related and can be confusing. Poor fuelling can have many knock-on effects so it is very important to adopt a methodical approach to diagnosis and rectification. Keep an eye out for air leaks anywhere in the system. If these occur on a modern closed-loop application such as this, the mixture will go rich. This is because the pressure to the MAP sensor is reduced which causes the management system to artificially richen the mixture. The presence of oil in the MAP sensor supply pipe can have the same effect. The Lambda sensor, in turn, fights against this but inevitably fails.

This condition can lead to the Lambda sensor becoming cont-

TECHNICAL SPECIFICATIONS

Toyota pin designation	Component	Output
G+	TDC sensor	Cranking 2V p/p+ Idle 10V p/p+
NE+	RPM sensor	Cranking 2V p/p+ Idle 10V p/p+
KNK	Knock sensor	1-2V p/p active
PIM	MAP sensor	Atmos. 3.5V Idle 1.5-1.7V
THA	Air temp. sensor	20°C 2-2.5V
OS	Oxygen sensor	hot 0.2-0.8V@1Hz+
THW	Coolant sensor	Cold 2-2.5V Hot 0.5-1V
VTA	Throttle pot.	Closed 0.3-0.5V Open 3.8-4.5V
IDL	Throttle switch	Closed 0.25V Open battery voltage
ISC	Idle control A/C	Active 1-3V Inactive NBV
RSC/RSO	Idle control	Ign. on 12V digital
	Injectors	Cold crank 4-6ms Cold idle 3.5-3.7ms Hot crank 2-4ms Hot idle 2-2.2ms All saturated pulse with 60V spike

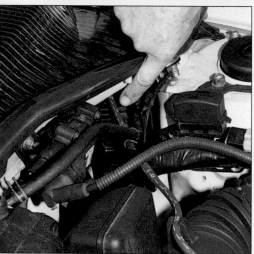
Air leaks anywhere in the system will spell drivability problems.

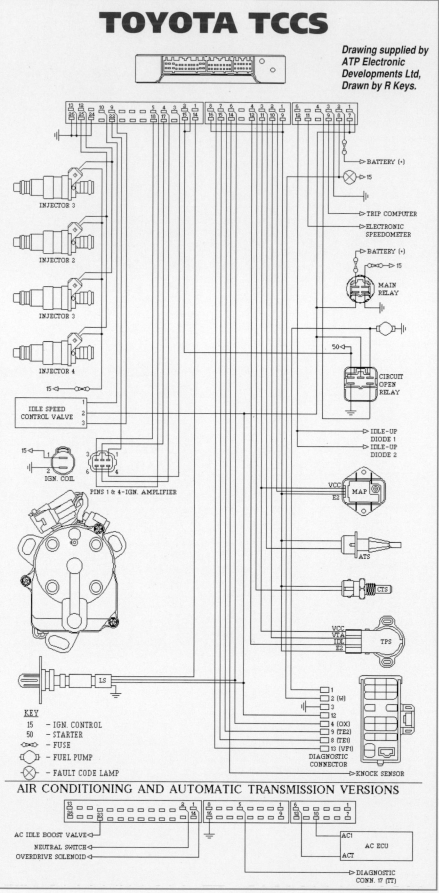

TOYOTA TCCS

Drawing supplied by ATP Electronic Developments Ltd, Drawn by R Keys.

INJECTOR 3

INJECTOR 2

INJECTOR 3

INJECTOR 4

IDLE SPEED CONTROL VALVE

IGN. COIL

PINS 1 & 4 – IGN. AMPLIFIER

LS

KEY
15 – IGN. CONTROL
50 – STARTER
⊶ – FUSE
⊏ – FUEL PUMP
⊗ – FAULT CODE LAMP

BATTERY (+)
15
TRIP COMPUTER
ELECTRONIC SPEEDOMETER
BATTERY (+)
15
MAIN RELAY
50
CIRCUIT OPEN RELAY
IDLE-UP DIODE 1
IDLE-UP DIODE 2
VCC E2 MAP
ATS
CTS
VCC VTA IDL E2 TPS

1
2 (W)
3
12
4 (OX)
9 (TE2)
8 (TE1)
13 (VF1)
DIAGNOSTIC CONNECTOR
KNOCK SENSOR

AIR CONDITIONING AND AUTOMATIC TRANSMISSION VERSIONS

AC IDLE BOOST VALVE
NEUTRAL SWITCH
OVERDRIVE SOLENOID

AC1
AC ECU
ACT
DIAGNOSTIC CONN. 17 (TT)

aminated with soot, a condition from which it is never likely to recover. Cleaning of the sensor is not really a viable option. Frank has tried but it doesn't work. The ceramic pocket inside is the problem. This is porous and once it becomes impregnated that is the end of the line. However, replacements are below £100 now so buying another shouldn't be the end of the world! Although Frank adds that they can be more if purchased from the dealer network.

Another problem Frank has come across is of engines which stall when hot. This relates to a fault with the coil (located within the distributor body) which breaks down with heat and goes 'open circuit'. A replacement coil should rectify the situation.

Finally, if you come across a car showing a high engine idle speed when hot, check the operation of the wax capsule-based idle control unit. There is a multiple idle control system on this car and the wax capsule is one part of it. This is effectively a 'cold only' valve which opens up an air passage when cold and closes it as the engine warms.

Check that this valve is fully closed when the engine is hot – the water temperature is obviously a crucial factor. It can be stripped for this purpose and manually operated, but if it still fails then replacements are available at reasonable prices.

NEXT MONTH
BMW 320i

ELECTRONIC DIAGNOSTICS!

Tracing and fixing faults in electronic engine management systems

Number 48: *The complex Bosch Motronic management systems used on later BMW models provide a challenge for the code-reader-only-equipped independent workshop. Chris Graham reports.*

Getting to grips with a modern BMW, from a diagnostics point of view, is not an easy business. Typical of the breed is the 320i 24v six-cylinder, with its Vanos variable cam timing mechanism.

The car is managed by a Bosch system called Motronic 3.3.1 which

POSSIBLE PROBLEMS
1. **Coolant sensor**
2. **Air mass meter**
3. **Crank angle sensor**

utilises an 88-pin ECU and provides total and sophisticated engine management. However, as Frank Massey,

proprietor at diagnostic and training specialist Fuel Injection Services (Tel: 01772 201597) points out, there are a number of Bosch variants used on different BMW applications, so it is important to be sure about exactly which you are dealing with.

This month we have decided to look

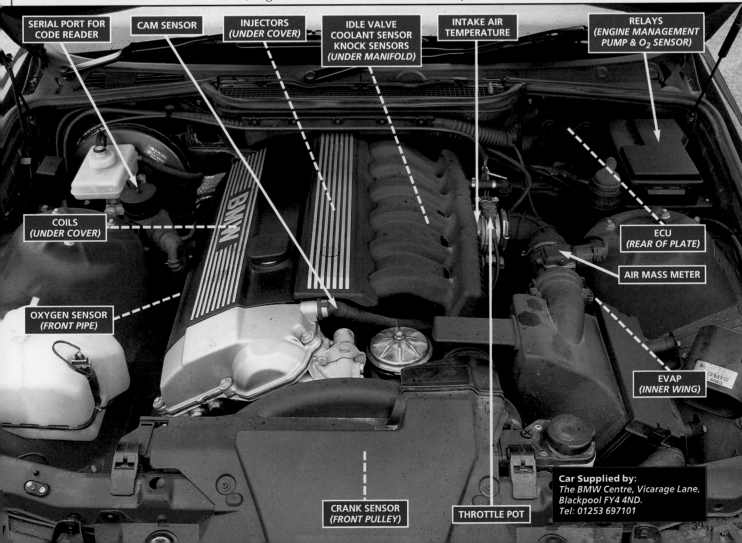

SERIAL PORT FOR CODE READER

CAM SENSOR

INJECTORS (UNDER COVER)

IDLE VALVE COOLANT SENSOR KNOCK SENSORS (UNDER MANIFOLD)

INTAKE AIR TEMPERATURE

RELAYS (ENGINE MANAGEMENT PUMP & O₂ SENSOR)

COILS (UNDER COVER)

ECU (REAR OF PLATE)

AIR MASS METER

OXYGEN SENSOR (FRONT PIPE)

EVAP (INNER WING)

CRANK SENSOR (FRONT PULLEY)

THROTTLE POT

Car Supplied by:
*The BMW Centre, Vicarage Lane, Blackpool FY4 4ND.
Tel: 01253 697101*

ENGINE MANAGEMENT

This Bosch 3.3.1 system provides total engine management with sequential injector control – each is controlled individually. Each of the six spark plugs has its own coil, and these are all controlled independently as well. This system of direct coil ignition enables a high level of control. Each cylinder can be controlled for knock purposes, for example, and should any one coil fail the relevant injector can be switched off to minimise emissions and prevent catalyst damage from unburnt fuel.

Other main components consist of: a crank angle sensor – which provides the key inputs to the ECU about engine speed and position; a camshaft phase sensor to aid injector timing; a coolant sensor; an ambient air sensor; a throttle potentiometer; a conventional titanium Lambda sensor; air bypass idle control rotary valve; a charcoal canister; six coils and injectors; a hot wire air mass meter; a pair of knock control sensors.

This engine also features variable camshaft timing, the purpose of which is to ensure good fuel economy around town, combined with good performance on the open road. One of the best features of this system is the speed at which it can work. The processing power of the ECU enhances response time enormously, resulting in a very finely controlled engine.

more at the problems associated with this car, from a code reading point of view. That is to say, approaching the job in the way that the less well equipped workshop is often forced to do.

First it is important to realise the advantages and disadvantages of a code reader. The plus points are that these units are affordable, easily connected and simple to use (prompt-driven testing from screen). On the downside, the information provided can be misleading and it is not possible to check all circuits.

At a practical level a code reader will obviously read codes and also clear them. It can also be used to drive certain actuators (fuel pump, injectors, ignition system etc.), to monitor and retrieve data (voltages, injector pulse times, ignition point etc.) and to clear service lights on this BMW application.

The key to successful code reader operation is interpretation. The unit may throw up a fault code relating to the coolant sensor, but all this tells you is that the fault could be with the sensor, the wiring or the ECU. It can be no more specific than this. The essential point to grasp is that what you are monitoring with a code reader is what is being 'seen' or calculated by the ECU. Everything presented needs to be qualified with careful thought and reason.

In most cases Frank considers that you will be able to rely on the code reader and succeed. But there will always be instances where confusion arises and you must be aware of this potential. The problem is that to check the findings of a code reader requires further investment, ideally in some form of oscilloscope. A conventional multimeter is of ever decreasing value in this respect. They simply cannot see certain spurious voltages and the rapid switching and glitches associated with diagnostics on modern vehicles.

PREPARATION

There is not a lot of preparation required with this engine. The most important area to concentrate on is around the coils. They are hidden behind plastic cosmetic panelling (as are

NEED TRAINING?
Frank Massey runs regular courses at his well-equipped Preston workshop; everything from basic engine management introductions to full-blown 'hands on', system-specific tuition.
Call 01772 201597 for details.

the injectors). There is no HT lead as such, but instead a long rubberised boot which extends down on to the plug directly from the coil.

These boots can lose their insulation quality with age, resulting in electrical tracking. It is crucial that this does not happen because it can cause damage within the ECU, and often does. They can be replaced independently of the coil so, if you find one that is obviously damaged or dirty, Frank's advice is to change all six.

The coils can suffer from deposits and contamination. If you find this and decide to wash them clean, then take special care to make sure they are dry before refitting. If the coil is faulty, and causing electrical tracking, the only solution is a replacement. Frank says that in his experience it is only usually the odd coil which needs changing.

Pin-pointing coil problems can be difficult without a quality oscilloscope.

Any misfires which may result will be incredibly quick and certainly way beyond the ability of any multimeter. Because there are no HT leads to connect to, the best way to tackle testing of this sort is to use a break-out box. In fact, Frank says that this is essential because of the general level of wiring inaccessibility on all modern BMWs.

It is important that the right type of spark plug is fitted, in terms of type of electrode, heat range and resistive element. The standard fit is a multi-electrode plug and it's perhaps best to stick with this.

There may be a need to wash out the idle control valve – this can suffer like any other but is not a common cause of problems. It is tucked away underneath the throttle body, lying along the side of the engine.

Cast an eye over the vacuum hoses and their connections. Air leaks will cause real problems but are not common under normal circumstances. However, there are a couple of hoses underneath the air inlet manifold which are a simple push fit. These can be popped off by backfires which may result from a coil problem. If this happens the car will go very rich.

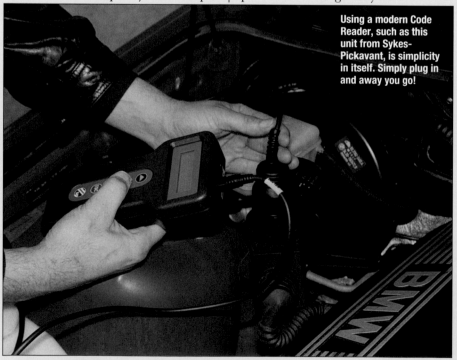

Using a modern Code Reader, such as this unit from Sykes-Pickavant, is simplicity in itself. Simply plug in and away you go!

ELECTRONIC DIAGNOSTICS!

TACKLING TROUBLE

Using a code reader can be a deceptive business. To be successful you will require a thorough knowledge of the vehicle, its management system and the interplay between components. There is plenty of scope for confusion.

The first example of this concerns the coolant sensor – a relatively common failure on this application. 'Lumpy' engine performance and a 'hunting' idle are the characteristic signs of this problem. When it occurs it usually fails to a 'cold' condition and the management system responds to this output by over-fuelling the engine. However, because the engine runs on closed loop emission control, the Lambda sensor will pick up this richness and send a signal back to the ECU for the fuelling to be leaned off. It will do this constantly and so its switching action will cease, and a fault code will be logged.

So plugging in your code reader will point you in the direction of a faulty Lambda sensor, when this is not actually the cause of the problem. Replacing it will achieve nothing. The root cause must be proved. The first approach might be to measure the injection pulse time. This can be done with the code reader and, if this proves to be correct, then the chances are that you are looking at a genuine Lambda sensor fault.

If you find that the injection pulse time is excessive, then you have to widen the search. Unfortunately, there are so many other sensors which could be having an effect. It may even be more than one. All you can do is work through the 'Equipment' listing checking each component against 'known data' as you go.

Often the value assigned to the coolant sensor will be in the form of an actual temperature, rather than a voltage. The two must correlate, so you will need to measure the voltage output at the back of the sensor and compare it with the temperature value being shown.

If the voltage is high (3.5V or so indicating a cool engine) and tallies with a 20°C temperature calculation from the ECU, as displayed by the code reader, then the ECU is working correctly and the fault lies with ei-

ECU on the 320i is tucked away behind this panel on the rear n/s of the engine bay.

ther the wiring or the sensor itself. But if the code reader displays 20°C and the coolant sensor voltage is just 0.5V (corresponding to a hot engine), then the ECU has made a mistake and is likely to be at fault internally.

Over-fuelling is a common problem on these cars and other typical causes can be an air leak in the inlet manifold or a fault with the air mass meter itself. The engine will always draw air from the easiest point and if it manages to bypass the air mass meter then you have a problem. Not only will extra air be being drawn in to fool the Lambda sensor into sending a 'go rich' signal, but also, the amount of air passing the air mass meter will be reduced, so this value will be corrupted too.

When using a code reader, this sort of complaint might be flagged as an air

mass meter fault or, once again, a problem with the lambda sensor. It may even signal that both are at fault. However, Frank believes that the chance of multiple components failing on this engine is slim. Generally the cause is one reacting to another, so careful thought and deduction is needed.

Check out the air mass meter with the code reader and assess the load value given. To do this effectively, of course, you need an accurate reference. It is unlikely that you will be able to find an 'official' provider but Frank says there are some good independent sources. He says that CAPS, the PC-based injection manual from Equiptech (Tel: 01703 862240) is very useful, and adds that the other, practical alternative is to take readings from a 'good' car.

Another area where code readers tend to be weak is when dealing with signal generators, such as crank angle sensors or camshaft phase sensors. These components generate an AC waveform and can only be effectively assessed using an oscilloscope if you intend to prove conclusively that a fault exists.

Having said this, the code reader is very effective at isolating a CAS-related fault in the first place. Crank angle sensor failure presents itself as a horrible misfire, an erratic tachometer needle, ignition and injector malfunctions and maybe even a complete engine failure.

This sensor provides the management system's prime trigger and so faults with it are heavily weighted as far as the code reader is concerned – which is why they are latched on to so effectively. Unfortunately,

TECHNICAL SPECIFICATIONS

Component	Voltage	ECM pin
Air mass meter	1.25-1.4V static 2.2-2.4V idle 4V+ snap	41
Throttle position indicator	0.5V closed 4.5V open	12
Coolant sensor	3.5V cold 0.8V hot	78
Inlet air temp sensor	Approx 2.4V hot	77
Crank angle sensor	Sine wave 20V p/p+ at idle	67
Camshaft position	Sine wave 20V p/p+ at idle	16
Injector duration	5.5ms cold 3.8ms hot 3ms cruise	3,4,5,31, 32,33
Coils	2.5ms burn time (view in primary)	23,24,25, 50,51,52
Idle control valve	12V digital 100Hz, 64% duty at hot idle 36% duty at hot idle	2 29
Evap	12V digital duty controlled variable	36
Lambda sensor	0.5-4.8V@1Hz+, hot	70

MONTRONIC 3.1.1

This wiring diagram is an example. Check in the relevant workshop manual for the diagram of the car you are working with.

Control unit Motronic 88

Battery

Ignition switch

Main relay

Speedometer

Air flow sensor

Pump relay

Fuel pump

Lambda sensor pre-heating

Throttle potentiometer

Air temperature sensor

Lambda sensor pre-heat. relay

Coolant temperature sensor

Injection valves

Ignition module

Camshaft sensor

Crankshaft sensor

Idle speed correction valve

Lambda sensor

Tank ventilation valve

Diagram courtesy of Autodiagnos. Tel: 01772 887774.

although the problem area is highlighted, insufficient information is provided to be conclusive about whether the fault is with the sensor or its immediate wiring.

The sensor takes its signal from a phonic wheel which rotates with the engine. This can become contaminated and suffer from dirt build-up. So the first and simplest move should always be to clean and check this and the sensor itself, to clear the stored code and re-test. If it continues to show a fault then replacement is the only solution.

Frank adds here that before you condemn any component you should always run through a basic check procedure. Assess the connection quality and bear in mind that the codes you have extracted may not be genuine. They could have been installed by a previous technician removing and replacing the components, for example.

Sometimes fault codes can be generated by HT interference. Coil breakdowns can be sufficient to spike the ECU, causing it to switch off for a fraction of a second. This can result in all sorts of fault codes being logged, including one relating to the ECU itself. The secret here, of course, is good preparation.

Generally, the ignition system is rather a closed book to a conventional code reader. However, because this system has the ability to close down an injector if and when a coil fails, the likely scenario is that the code reader will home in on the 'silenced' injector as being the problem.

Remember that the code reader can only ever pass on to you what the ECU is telling it. Think of the ECU as a computer – feed rubbish in and you will get rubbish out!

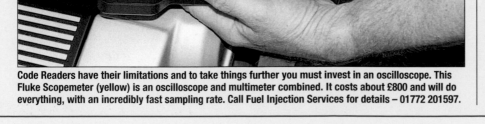

Code Readers have their limitations and to take things further you must invest in an oscilloscope. This Fluke Scopemeter (yellow) is an oscilloscope and multimeter combined. It costs about £800 and will do everything, with an incredibly fast sampling rate. Call Fuel Injection Services for details – 01772 201597.

NEXT MONTH
Audi A3/A4

ELECTRONIC DIAGNOSTICS!

Tracing and fixing faults in electronic engine management systems

Number 49: *The state-of-the-art engine management system used on Audi's new A3 has plenty of refinement, but what about its future reliability? Chris Graham investigates.*

The Bosch Motronic 3.8.2 system used on the latest Audi A3 1.8 turbo is one of many versions of this reliable management package found across the range of German saloons and many other vehicle applications besides.

The system is complex and dealing

LIKELY FAULTS
1. **Idle switch**
2. **Misfires**
3. **Injectors**

with it successfully requires skilled interpretation of information provided by relatively expensive diagnostic

equipment. Frank Massey, proprietor and training expert at Preston-based Fuel Injection Services (Tel: 01772 201597) is a firm believer in the professional approach. He says that to gather worthwhile data from these modern systems is getting difficult, although there is still a basic code read-

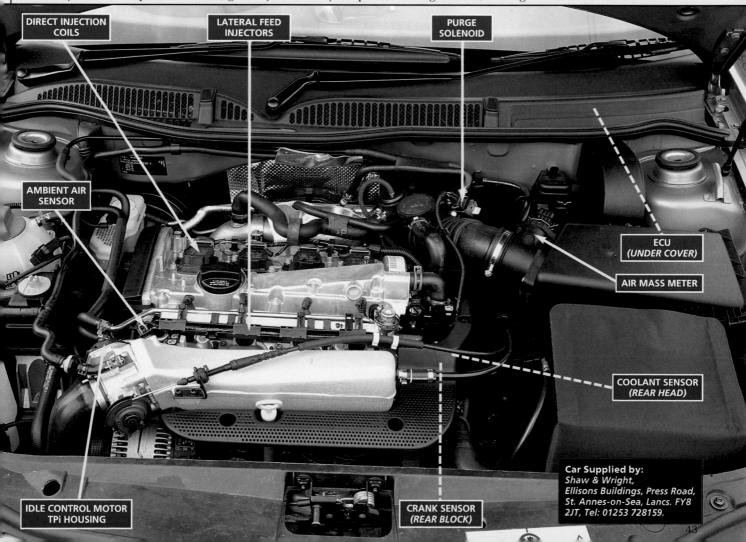

DIRECT INJECTION COILS

LATERAL FEED INJECTORS

PURGE SOLENOID

AMBIENT AIR SENSOR

ECU (UNDER COVER)

AIR MASS METER

COOLANT SENSOR (REAR HEAD)

IDLE CONTROL MOTOR TPi HOUSING

CRANK SENSOR (REAR BLOCK)

Car Supplied by:
Shaw & Wright,
Ellisons Buildings, Press Road,
St. Annes-on-Sea, Lancs. FY8
2JT, Tel: 01253 728159.

ENGINE MANAGEMENT

This Bosch Motronic system has many similarities to earlier versions that we have covered in the past. In common with many other modern vehicles, Audi have opted for direct ignition on this application, with one coil per cylinder. There are many reasons for this, one of which is the increasing need to be able to monitor any emission-related failures. To achieve this effectively, the spark must be monitored accurately and the best way to do this is by studying individual ignition performance.

The system operates with multipoint injection with laterally-fed fuel injectors. Most components are very 'traditional' and include: a coolant temperature sensor; an ambient air temperature sensor; a pair of knock sensors; a crank angle sensor to provide engine speed and position information; a Hall sensor which is effectively a camshaft ID sensor; an impressive throttle body assembly (denoted as TVU assembly) which contains the stepper motor for controlling engine idle, an idle contact and a dual throttle potentiometer assembly.

There is an oxygen sensor; a hot film air flow sensor (load device); a variable camshaft timing system (dependent upon vehicle spec.) which is operated by a relatively simple electro-hydraulic solenoid. It is active between about 1,800 and 3,600rpm and acts effectively as a torque control device; a crankcase ventilation valve to allow HCs to be drawn back into the air intake; an in-tank fuel pump and a fuel pump relay.

The fault code socket, for accessing the system, is found in the centre of the dash, behind a small trim panel. This is in common with most modern VW/Audi applications now. However, on a more general note, it should be pointed out that accessibility on this engine to some of the components is difficult, which increases the problems associated with taking direct measurements.

The ECU is located close to the wiper motor, at the back of the engine bay, within the bulkhead. It features two separate sockets, in common with many other modern applications.

ing capability available.

However, as we mentioned last time, the limitation with a code reader is that only certain circuits can be monitored and the information which is gathered tends to centre around sensor outputs. This is fine as far as it goes, but does nothing to assist with the tracking down of ground faults or problems with relays etc. To achieve this you must take things a stage further by venturing into the world of parallel snapshot interfacing!

Adopting this technique allows you to 'break into' the system between the ECU and the vehicle loom, so that all the inputs, the power-ups and the earths, plus the actuator outputs, can be monitored at a speed which is infinitely faster than with a code reader. So even the fastest 'spurious' fault can be logged – the quickest glitch – and all this can be achieved while actually road testing the car which gives the whole process complete realism. No operation of the handset during testing is required and faults are notified by a beep.

All the data recorded is stored in a handset and can be downloaded to a PC if required once testing is complete. The piece of equipment which Frank recommends for this advanced form of diagnostics is the Swedish-made Multitester-Plus, which is available exclusively from Autodiagnos UK Ltd (Tel: 01772 887774).

This machine does not present its findings on screen. It compares everything it records with known values stored on the computer chip (one for each management system). However, you can view 'live data' and scroll through the ECU pins to watch actual values, in terms of milliseconds, switching frequency, voltage – whatever is appropriate. It is also possible to carry out 'special checks' which can be useful once the fault has been narrowed down to a specific component. Every-

thing can be focused to the operation of just one component for a thorough assessment.

Faults are logged, together with a 'snapshot' of other factors such as the speed of the engine, water temperature, injection duration etc., at the instant it occured. You are then guided to more specific testing of that component/circuit. However, intellegent interpretation by the operator is still required. A logged fault with ECU pin one could still relate to the wiring, the component or the ECU – the technician must decide.

PREPARATION

Because this is still such a new system there is not a great deal to be said about preparation. Generally, Frank was impressed with the layout of the engine and he believes that the various plastic covers and 'fake' manifolds used may well help keep the engine clean and free from contamination in the long run. The quality of the engineering looks good too and he has little doubt that the car will wear well.

However, as always, you must remove the plugs, even though in this case the individual coils have to be removed too. Franks says be sure to make the effort because plugs provide a tremendously valuable 'window' into what is actually happening within the engine.

Be careful when removing the coil because the plug extension which runs down into the head can be sensitive to bending. It probably contains a ceramic section which is easily cracked. When you inspect the plugs watch for the presence of what Frank describes as a 'corona ring' around the base of the porcelain section – a brownish staining. This is a sure indicator of 'flash over' and shows that there has been electrical tracking on the outside of the plug and running to ground.

If you find this then you will more than likely have to replace the plug extensions. The condition can lead to misfires and hesitation so it is important to take the correct action at the

Battery is insulated and electrically protected on this Audi A3 application.

ELECTRONIC DIAGNOSTICS!

preparation stage. Frank believes that the extensions are now available separately from the coil, which helps keep costs down. Make sure, as always, that the correct type of plug is fitted and that their apertures are clean and dry.

Because the idle control mechanism is built into the throttle body on this application, this can no longer be accessed for cleaning. Frank does not recommend submerging the whole body in cleaning solution, because it contains two potentiometers and a micro switch. Unfortunately, problems here tend to mean replacement of the complete body, which will be expensive.

Check all the vacuum hoses for kinking general deterioration. Because this is a closed loop system, any air leaks will lead directly to fuelling problems.

FUTURE PROBLEMS

Because of the newness of this Audi application, it is too early to say definitely where any problems will strike for sure. However, Frank's experience suggests that most trouble tends to occur with components that move.

On several ocassions he has come across a problem with a similar throttle body arrangement, but on a different vehicle. It related specifically to 'noise' across the idle switch and this condition has to be confirmed with the use of an oscilloscope because you are looking at an erratic switching of voltage.

The trouble is caused by the ECU's interpretation of this erratic signal. In an ideal world the control unit likes things simple. It wants to 'see' either an 'open' or a 'closed' signal – that's the whole point of having a switch. But if the switch contacts become dirty or contaminated the switching action gets electrically blurred, giving the impression to the ECU that the driver is continually on and off the throttle. This is translated into hesitant engine performance as the over-run fuel cut-off and idle control mechanisms are repeatedly switched. This can lead to an erratic idle also, surging while driving and maybe even stalling.

It's an easy condition to check, assuming you have an oscilloscope. You will have to

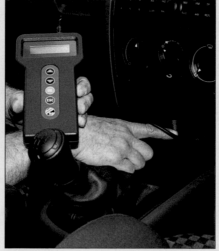

Code reader socket is found in the centre console, at the back of a small oddments compartment ahead of the gearlever.

make and break the contact several times so that the voltage switch quality can be assessed. With the scope you will be able to see the voltage change from a horizontal to a vertical direction, as the switch occurs. This must be visibly clean – just a single line with no tell-tale signal interference indicating 'noise' or hash.

The potentiometers within the throttle body could well suffer in a similar way. They rely on a clean electrical track for their precise operation and output accuracy. Problems here will cause similar drivability problems with the possible addition of flat spots for good measure!

Unfortunately, the design of the throttle body makes it impossible to get at the idle switch or the potentiome-

ters, for cleaning purposes. All you can really do is to prove where the problem lies and then seek a replacement unit. However, as a last ditch effort, Frank says that it is always worth trying a 'condemned' body in an ultrasonic cleaning tank if possible.

This really is a kill or cure step but, if you've proved the component to be 'dead' in the first place, you have nothing to lose and everything to gain. It might just work, and save a lot of money!

Another potential problem is plug-related and one we have touched on already. 'Flash over' across the porcelain section of one or more spark plugs can cause very noticeable performance defects.

Because these systems have such a high output nowadays – 60,000-70,000V is not unusual – insulation weaknesses are sort out and exploited. There is so much power there that anything which presents an easier route to earth will be taken. The problem is that to find a misfire of this type is very difficult, even with an oscilloscope. Often the amount of energy required by the spark for it to traverse the outside of the plug and leak away to earth can be exactly the same as it takes to jump the gap in the normal way. When this is the case there will be no evidence of the problem when voltages are checked with the oscilloscope.

The only reliable way to spot the problem is with a careful visual inspection. At the first sign of any discolouration on the

THE SERIES SO FAR

BASIC SYSTEMS – July 1994 DIAGNOSTIC EQUIPMENT – August 1994 TEST PREPARATION – September 1994 FORD 2.0i – October 1994 ROVER 200/400 – November 1994 VAUXHALL 2.0i – December 1994 PEUGEOT 205/309 GTi – January 1995 FORD 2.9i V6 – February 1995 BMW 1.8i – March 1995 VAUXHALL 2.0i 16V – April 1995 ROVER 2.0i 16V – May 1995 ROVER 1.6/2.0 EFi – June 1995 ROVER 1.6/2.0 IGNITION – July 1995 FORD ZETA 16V – August 1995 VW 1.8 DIGIFANT – September 1995 HONDA LEGEND/ROVER 800 – October 1995 FORD XR2i/RS TURBO – November 1995 PEUGEOT 405 Mi16 – December 1995 RENAULT CLIO 1.2i – January 1996 VAUXHALL 24V – February 1996 RANGE ROVER V8 – March 1996 HONDA CIVIC 1.6 – April 1996 ROVER 820 SINGLE POINT – May 1996 JAGUAR 3.6 STRAIGHT SIX – June 1996 AUDI 80 – July 1996 FORD ESCORT/FIESTA – August 1996 VAUXHALL 1.8i – September 1996 SAAB 900/9000 – November 1996 VW DIGIFANT UPDATE – December 1996 VAUXHALL ECOTEC – January 1997 NISSAN MICRA 16V – February 1997 PEUGEOT 1.8i – March 1997 VOLVO 940 2.0 – April 1997 FIAT PUNTO 1.2 – May 1997 BMW 24V – June 1997 CITROEN AX – July 1997 NISSAN PRIMERA – August 1997 RENAULT LAGUNA 2.0 – September 1997 MGF – October 1997 ESCORT COSWORTH – November 1997 CITROEN XANTIA – December 1997 VAUXHALL 1.4i – January 1998 FORD EEC V 1.25 – February 1998 VAUXHALL 2.5 V6 – March 1998 VW SIMOS – April 1998 ROVER 600 – May 1998 TOYOTA CARINA E – June 1998 BMW 3-SERIES – July 1998.

TECHNICAL SPECIFICATIONS

Component	Voltage	ECM pin
Crank angle sensor	Sinewave – Cranking 2V+ Idle 11V+ Cruise 14V	56/63
Camshaft ID	Digital 5V/0V	76
Throttle assembly	Stepper 0-5V	66/59
	Idle contact 12-0V closed	69
	Throt. pos. 0.5-4.5V WOT	75
	Sensor supply 5V+	62
	Throt. pos. 0.5-4.5V WOT	74
Coolant sensor	0.5V hot, 3.5V cold	53
Air temp. sensor	2.8-3.2V @ 20°C	54
Knock sensor 1	A/C 1-2.5V active	60
Knock sensor 2	A/C 1-2.5V active	68
Lambda sensor	0.3-0.7V	26
Variable cam timing	12-1.25V	55
Charcoal canister	Duty and frequency modified 12-0V	15
Fuel injectors	Crank cold 11+ms	(1) 73
	Crank hot 4+ms	(2) 80
	Idle cold 3-3.5ms	(3) 58
	Idle hot 2-2.5ms	(4) 65
	Snap 6.0ms	
Air flow meter	1.5-3.5V snap	13
Ignition trigger	12V digital	71/78
Speed sensor	12V digital	20

MONTRONIC 3.8.2

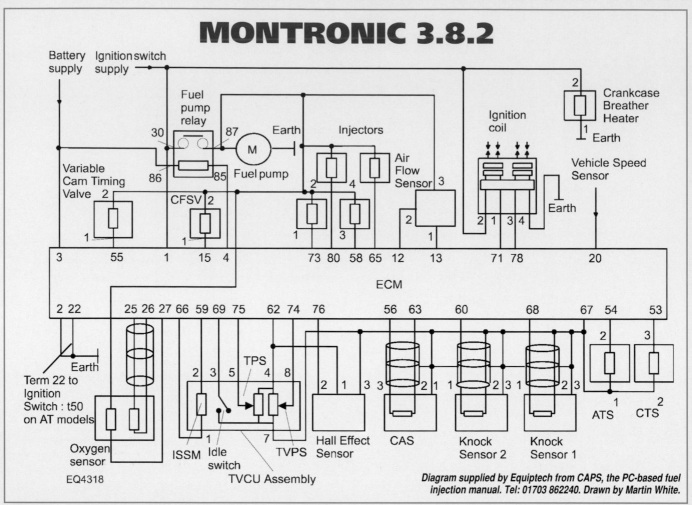

Battery supply | Ignition switch supply

Fuel pump relay

30 | 87 | Earth

86 | 85 | Fuel pump | M

Variable Cam Timing Valve | 2 | 1

CFSV | 2 | 1

Injectors | 2 | 4

Air Flow Sensor | 3

1 | 3

2 | 1

Ignition coil

2 | 1 | 3 | 4

Earth

Crankcase Breather Heater | 2 | 1 | Earth

Vehicle Speed Sensor | Earth

3 | 55 | 1 | 15 | 4 | 73 | 80 | 58 | 65 | 12 | 13 | 71 | 78 | 20

ECM

2 | 22 | 25 | 26 | 27 | 66 | 59 | 69 | 75 | 62 | 74 | 76 | 56 | 63 | 60 | 68 | 67 | 54 | 53

Earth

Term 22 to Ignition Switch : t50 on AT models

Oxygen sensor | EQ4318

ISSM | Idle switch

TPS | 2 | 3 | 5 | 4 | 8

1 | 7

TVPS

TVCU Assembly

Hall Effect Sensor | 2 | 1 | 3

CAS | 3 | 2 | 1

Knock Sensor 2 | 1 | 2 | 3

Knock Sensor 1 | 1 | 2 | 3

ATS | 2 | 1

CTS | 3 | 2

Diagram supplied by Equiptech from CAPS, the PC-based fuel injection manual. Tel: 01703 862240. Drawn by Martin White.

body of a plug, change it and the coil extension too. As a general rule Frank would replace plugs and extensions as a complete set – he advises that the latter cost about £10 each.

Another possible stumbling block for the future concerns the injectors. Their laterally-fed configuration means that the role played by the upper and lower fluid seals is vital. They can suffer badly from careless handling, being easily nipped or trapped during fitting. Alternatively, with age they can harden and lose their sealing ability.

Quite often a fuel leak past the bottom seal will remain undetected simply because there is nothing to see. The fuel is disappearing straight into the engine to produce excess fuelling that will be picked up by the Lambda sensor. This will send the appropriate 'go lean' signal to the ECU and fuel supply will be reduced across all four injectors. This could then result in the strange situation where the cylinder with the leaking injector actually shows correct fuelling, while the other three are all running lean! Upon whipping the plugs out you may well see three lean and one normal... Think before you act! The symptoms, from the driver's point of view, will be a flat engine with very poor acceleration because fuelling will have been reduced. There may also be evidence of pinking if the engine is running hot.

The other potential catch is that when you attempt a pressure proof test, which you carry out by crimping the fuel line, the leak remains 'invisible'. Once again, careful visual inspection often wins the day. Remove the injectors and examine the O ring seals for any cuts or signs of poor fitting and distortion. The injectors can, of course, be tested by a specialist with the right equipment – Frank has an Asnu flow bench with a purpose-made mounting rail for pressure testing laterally-fed injectors.

The simple solution to damaged seals is to replace them. They are available separately but must be fitted carefully. Never use grease because this may become deposited on the injector pintel head. It may also harden with heat. Frank's advice is to use a light lubricant such as WD40 spray to ensure they are fitted without damage.

The Autodiagnos Multitester-Plus and interface. Handset costs about £2,500, breakout box with the software pods cost about £200 each and you will require one of these per managament system. It should be stressed that these are system-based pods which will operate across manufacturer 'boundaries'. So the Bosch Motronic pod will be suited to many applications from BMW, Citroen, Alfa Romeo, Vauxhall etc.

NEXT MONTH
Mazda 626

ELECTRONIC DIAGNOSTICS!

Tracing and fixing faults in electronic engine management systems

Number 50: *The Mazda 626 has an excellent reputation for build quality and overall durability. Top of the range is the tempting V6 version. It's a refined performer but what of its mechanical and electrical reliability? Chris Graham finds out.*

attended the launch of the re-vamped Mazda 626 in sunny Florida, back in 1991. I can re-member then being impressed with the car, particularly the gutsy yet smooth 2.5-litre V6 model. Now, some seven years later, I still have the car ear-marked as a potential, value for money long-legged cruiser.

To discover just how good the vehi-cle still is, I paid a visit to Mazda main agent Whichford, Reading (Tel: 01189 871278), in the expert company of Simon Ashby from fuel injection spe-cialists RA Engineering (Tel: 01189 571369). Simon bravely volunteered to step into Frank Massey's shoes this month, while Frank takes a well earned break in the Costa del Diagnostics!

LIKELY FAULTS
1. **High emissions**
2. **Lambda sensor**
3. **Throttle pot.**

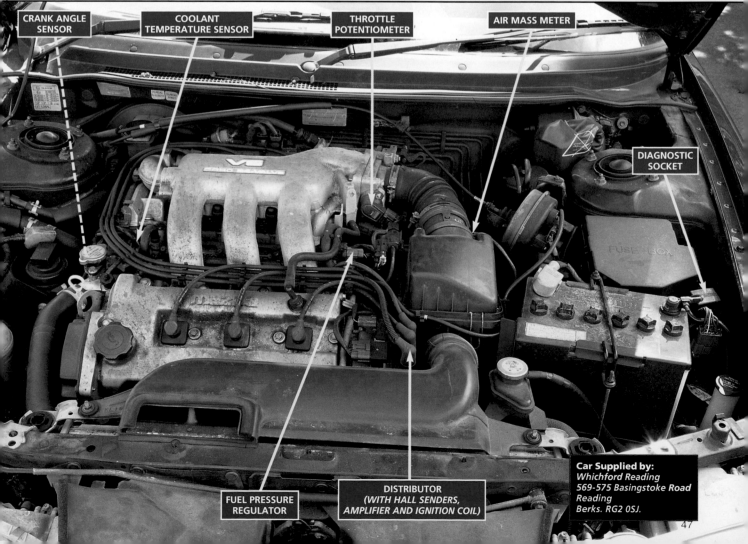

CRANK ANGLE SENSOR

COOLANT TEMPERATURE SENSOR

THROTTLE POTENTIOMETER

AIR MASS METER

DIAGNOSTIC SOCKET

FUEL PRESSURE REGULATOR

DISTRIBUTOR (WITH HALL SENDERS, AMPLIFIER AND IGNITION COIL)

Car Supplied by:
Whichford Reading
569-575 Basingstoke Road
Reading
Berks. RG2 0SJ.

ENGINE MANAGEMENT

The system runs multi-port sequential fuel injection and is governed by a single ECU (found in the centre console within the car). This responds to an inductive trigger. Idle speed and ignition timing are adjustable but CO levels are not.

Major system components and features include: an integrated intake air temperature sensor; a pair of four-wire Lambda sensors, which are heated (one on each, bank, located in the downpipes); a distributor containing two Hall triggers; an external ignition amplifier; a throttle valve potentiometer with an integrated idle control switch; an auxiliary air device to assist with cold starting – a temperature sensitive wax-based valve; idle speed control valve.

An atmospheric pressure sensor within the ECU; a crank angle sensor; a vacuum solenoid for regulating fuel supply pressure to the actual regulator; a variable induction system for performance enhancement operated by an internal flap within the inlet manifold; a full closed loop system including purge control valve for dealing with fuel vapour from the tank; a coolant temperature sensor; an intake fuel pump; an inertia switch located in the boot; full limp home mode.

There is a code reading potential on this system but it is best tackled using an LED test lamp. To initiate this, one side of the LED is connected to battery positive, while the other is attached to the terminal marked 'FEN' within the diagnostic socket, on the nearside inner wing close to the battery.

You then have to establish a jump link between the terminals 'GND' and 'TEN', and follow this by switching on the ignition. At this point, any stored fault codes – and there are potentially 38 of these, although only 13 can be stored in the system – will be displayed by a sequence of flashing with intervals in between. Simon says that it may well take a few goes before you can make any sense of the flashing. The spacing between codes is subtle (tens and units are obviously presented one after the other) and you should consult your equipment manufacturer for assistance with this if you experience any difficulty. It's not an ideal system but the codes displayed are usually accurate, so it's well worth persevering.

As far as code readers are concerned, the availability of software pods is rather limited, although Simon knows for a fact that the Bosch KTS 300 unit will interrogate this system effectively.

The management system used on this Mazda application is called MECS (Mazda Engine Control System). The same engine is used in the MX-6 model and also on V6 variants of Ford's Probe. Consequently, it also appears to be known under other assorted designations including EGI and VRIS! There do not seem to be any specific version designations and no significant system variations between models, according to Simon.

As with most Japanese based systems, this one is essentially very reliable, assuming an adequate level of maintenance and servicing. Under the bonnet the installation is very tight, in common with most modern V6 applications these days. The standard of engineering is generally high and so the prospects for overall longevity look encouraging. Certainly, the dealer feedback we received about reliability levels was very promising.

PREPARATION

As ever with vehicle preparation prior to effective fault diagnostics, checking the integrity of the ignition system must be one of your prime objectives, particularly if you suspect there are problems with the injection system.

By and large, this engine has a reputation for remaining relatively clean. The example here had covered about 56,000 miles and, while generally grubby, looked in pretty good shape.

Carry out all the basic checks at this stage. Inspect the condition of the HT leads and check also that the right plugs are fitted and are correctly gapped.

Pay attention to all sensor connectors and plugs, particularly those which may have thrown up a fault code. Dirty connections can be at the root of many an apparently mysterious fault. Check also the condition of the various vacuum hoses around the engine.

There are some, which run close to the rear inlet manifold, which could be a potential source of future trouble. It is also a sensible move to clear the fault code memory, and then run the vehicle again to re-establish exactly what the problem might be. Always remember, you never know who has been fiddling with the vehicle before you – and what they may have disconnected. Perfectly serviceable sensors can be logged as faulty in this way, so Simon advises clearing the lot and carrying out a test drive to establish the true extent of the problem – assuming the vehicle is a runner of course!

Air Mass Meter.

ELECTRONIC DIAGNOSTICS!

TROUBLE IN STORE!

The seemingly inherent reliability of these Japanese applications always makes this section of these features tricky. The cars are just too damn good! All we can reasonably do is point you in the direction of potential problems which might occur given time and mileage.

The first problem Simon detailed – and this is one he has come across on MX-6 variants – relates to the HT leads. The practical symptoms are a slightly poor idle, a misfire during acceleration and, perhaps most conclusively, a very high HC emission level – often in excess of 1,000ppm. The root of the problem is electrical tracking on one of the plug leads.

Usually this will have been caused by nothing more than straightforward ageing. The rubber, particularly on the section which extends down into the head and over the plug, becomes hardened and more prone to splitting and cracking. It gradually loses its insulative qualities until the point is reached when it is easier for the spark to jump to the adjacent cylinder head than to proceeded down to the plug.

Locating the offending lead is simplified by the fact that you can disconnect the injectors one bank at a time. Simon would recommend that you always replace the lead and the plug when this type of fault is discovered.

Without the aid of an oscilloscope for identifying the troublesome lead, the only solution is careful visual inspection. The damage is usually visible with the naked eye and, at least, using this method you are sure of the cause.

Another possible cause of trouble can stem from Lambda sensor failure or performance deterioration. While this may well trigger the dashboard warning light, there may be few other signs of trouble. The 'limp home' mode on this vehicle is so effective that many motorists will be unaware that it has been activated at all. There is very little deterioration in performance, although the cost conscious may well spot an increase in fuel consumption.

This tends, in most cases, to be an age-related problem. Most commonly the switching action becomes 'lazy' – it slows down.

Coolant temperature sensor.

The practical result of this is a slight but noticeable 'hunting' while driving the vehicle on a constant throttle. Gentle surging will be obvious as the sensor switches slowly, and the engine reacts by accelerating and then decelerating.

Replacement of the faulty sensor really is the only solution. Simon says that there are a number of manufacturers now providing perfectly good equipment into the aftermarket. He says, for example, that Lucas now produce a very competitively priced range of one, two, three and four-wire Lambda sensors. He uses these often and finds their performance excellent.

This engine, of course, is fitted with two Lambda sensors so you are faced with the dilemma of whether or not to replace them both. It is certainly good workshop practice to replace both components at the same time but, obviously, the financial aspects are important for many owners. The chances are that once one fails, the other won't be far behind. If, on the other hand, the problem evidently relates to a wiring or connector problem on just one sensor, then replacement of the other one is probably not necessary.

All moving parts eventually wear out – there is no escaping that fact. One component which suffers in this way, to cause real drivability problems, is the throttle potentiometer. If the idle switch becomes faulty then the result of this can be a noticeably higher fuel consumption, because over-run fuel cut off will not be operating effectively.

A fault on the throttle potentiometer track itself will generate flat spots in certain throttle positions. The variable output from the pot. should be easily distinguishable using an oscilloscope, and will normally occur at the lower end of the rev range simply because it is this section which receives the most use.

In some cases you can diagnose this type of problem using a voltmeter, but Simon admits that this is beyond the scope of most types, particularly those with digital readouts, which tend to fluctuate rapidly at the best of times in units of 100s!

The bad news is that the throttle potentiometer track cannot be cleaned effectively – it is a completely sealed unit and so, unfortunately, replacement is the only viable repair option. Simon believes the cost of new units is about £50.

TECHNICAL SPECIFICATIONS

Component	Voltage/resistance	ECM pin
Throttle pot.	0V closed, 12V open	1T
	0.5V closed rising smoothly as throttle opens	2F
Coolant temp. sens.	3.5V cold, 0.5V hot	2E
Crank angle sensor	500-600ohms	3F-3H
Fuel injectors	12-16ohms each	n/a
Solenoid valve for pressure regulator	30-50ohms	3M-1B
Lambda sensors	0-1V oscillating	2D-2C
Idle actuator	10-15ohms	3Q-1B
Hall senders	12V square wave	3E-3G
Injector durations	Approx. 2.5ms at idle with engine hot	3U
		3V
	Initial cold start 6-8ms	3W
		3X
		3Y
		3Z

NEXT MONTH
VW Golf TDi.

MAZDA ENGINE CONTROL SYSTEM

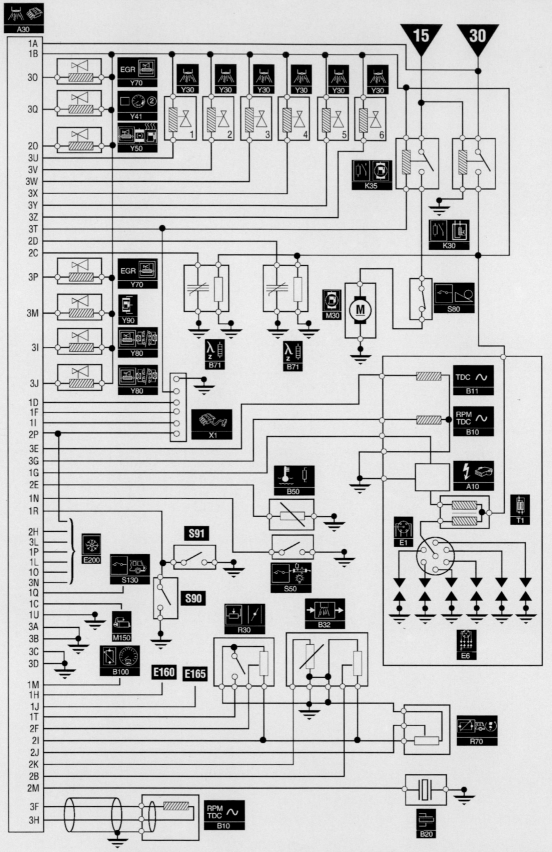

Diagram supplied by Equiptech from CAPS, the PC-based fuel injection manual. Tel: 01703 862240. Drawn by Martin White.

KEY

15. IGNITION FEED
30. BATTERY & FEED
Y90. SOLENOID VALVE FOR FUEL PRESSURE REGULATION
Y41. IDLE ACTUATOR
Y30. INJECTORS
Y70. EXHAUST GAS RECIRCULATION VALVE x2

Y50. PURGE CONTROL VALVE
K35. FUEL PUMP RELAY
K30. MAIN RELAY
S80. INERTIA SWITCH
M30. FUEL PUMP
B71. LAMBDA SENSORS
Y80. SOLENOID VALVES FOR VARIABLE INDUCTION SYSTEM x2
X1. DIAGNOSTIC SOCKET

B10 & B11. HALL SENSORS
B10 (3F & 3H). CRANK ANGLE SENSOR
B32. AIR MASS METER
B50. COOLANT TEMPERATURE SENSOR
A10. IGNITION AMPLIFIER
B30. THROTTLE POTENTIOMETER
S130. BRAKE LIGHT SWITCH
B100. INSTRUMENT CLUSTER

E160. BACK-UP LAMPS
E165. HEATED REAR WINDOW
S50. POWER STEERING PRESSURE SWITCH
R70. EGR POSITION SENSOR
T1. COIL
S90 & 91. P/N SWITCH & CLUTCH SWITCH
M150. STARTER MOTOR
E200. AIR CONDITIONING

affordable technology
with a proven track record....

.... from Sykes-Pickavant
the specialist in automotive service tools.

For your free copy of our
52 page Workshop Catalogue
ring 01253 783400 NOW!

Sykes-Pickavant Ltd. Kilnhouse Lane, Lytham St Annes, Lancashire, FY8 3DU.

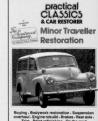

ELECTRONIC DIAGNOSTICS!

Tracing and fixing faults in electronic engine management systems

Number 51: *This month we take our first and long-awaited look at the diagnostic delicacies of a modern diesel engine. Volkswagen's popular Golf provides the motor, Chris Graham chooses the words.*

Most modern diesels operate on the direct injection principal these days, because it provides superior fuel economy and better power output. The system is generally more suited to the use of turbochargers and cylinder heads are cheaper to manufacture too.

LIKELY FAULTS
1. **Needle lift sensor**
2. **Crank angle sensor**
3. **Injection pump**

We all know how durable modern diesels tend to be, but what of their electronic reliability? The latest examples are literally bristling with state-of-the-art control systems and, in many ways they are more complicated and trickier to deal with than the equivalent petrol models. For some answers I ventured north of the border to visit independent electronic diagnostic expert William McLaren (Tel: 0370 737257).

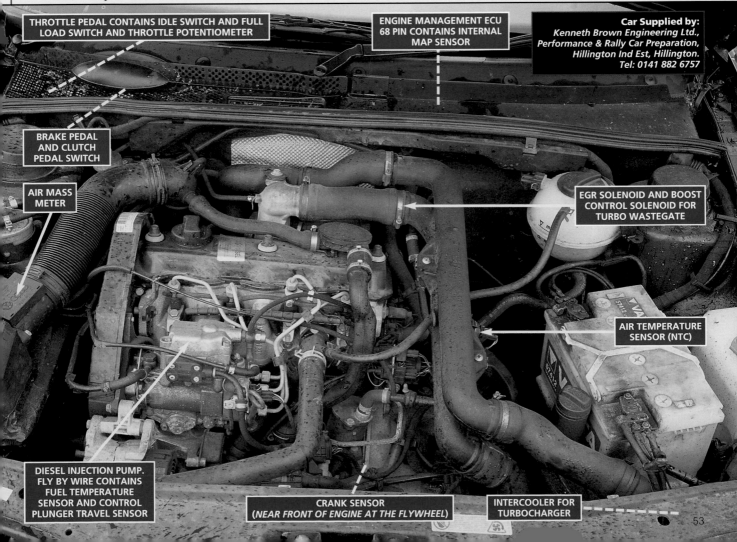

THROTTLE PEDAL CONTAINS IDLE SWITCH AND FULL LOAD SWITCH AND THROTTLE POTENTIOMETER

ENGINE MANAGEMENT ECU 68 PIN CONTAINS INTERNAL MAP SENSOR

Car Supplied by:
Kenneth Brown Engineering Ltd.,
Performance & Rally Car Preparation,
Hillington Ind Est, Hillington.
Tel: 0141 882 6757

BRAKE PEDAL AND CLUTCH PEDAL SWITCH

AIR MASS METER

EGR SOLENOID AND BOOST CONTROL SOLENOID FOR TURBO WASTEGATE

AIR TEMPERATURE SENSOR (NTC)

DIESEL INJECTION PUMP. FLY BY WIRE CONTAINS FUEL TEMPERATURE SENSOR AND CONTROL PLUNGER TRAVEL SENSOR

CRANK SENSOR
(NEAR FRONT OF ENGINE AT THE FLYWHEEL)

INTERCOOLER FOR TURBOCHARGER

ENGINE MANAGEMENT

This Golf TDi 1.9-litre is managed by a Seimens ECU with 68 pins. It features internal MAP sensing to measure boost pressure, together with full EGR and emission control so there is no idle adjustment potential. The same engine and management system is used by the Passat, plus other selected models in the SEAT range and the Ford Galaxy.

The ECU is located below the windscreen and so can suffer from water ingress. Its connectors can suffer too, giving poor drivability and suggesting, to the unitiated, a problem with the pump. Be warned!

Primary components in this system include: an air mass meter; an air temperature sensor; a fuel temperature sensor; a fuel quantity sensor; a fly-by-wire electronic throttle pedal; a diesel injection pump which contains a multitude of electronics but is not serviceable; a fully closed loop emission control system; a crankshaft position sensor; a needle lift sensor, which is housed within No.3 injector. The function of this is to inform the ECU when this cylinder is firing and, together with the crank angle sensor, it provides the primary trigger for the system.

There is a 'limp home' mode, which sets a faster then normal idle speed (up to 1,200-1,400rpm) and reduces overall engine performance – signified by the lighting of the glowplug light on the dash. This is unusual as there is no specific engine management warning light on this system. The ECU is programmed with back-up settings for most of the major components in the system.

If a major failure is detected, then the control unit has the power to close down the whole system to protect the engine. The pump will be stopped by cutting the fuel supply.

At present, William says that there are no aftermarket code readers which are able to interrogate this system. Both Ford and Volkswagen use their own dealer-only systems for fault diagnosis. He says the best approach for the independent is to access the system at the ECU, using a suitable adaptor and a breakout box. William is in a fortunate position because, having an electronics background, he is able to manufacture his own connectors.

By and large, this system is very reliable, assuming a good level of maintenance and a tamper-free life. Mechanical work carried out carelessly can lead to problems, particularly if earth straps are left disconnected.

William is a rare character because he is one of the few tuning and fault-finding specialists with the necessary knowledge and experience to deal competently with diesels. I met him at a windswept and damp Glasgow airport, and we set off to track down our 'guinea pig' Golf.

On route he started to explain about the high cost of most diesel components, emphasising the importance of correct diagnosis if bills are to be kept within reason. With diesel pumps costing £1,500+ and replacement ECUs £1,000 to buy, careless thinking really can cost a fortune.

In general, most components from a diesel are two or three times as expensive as the petrol equivalent. So, although problems are relatively rare, when they do strike they can be both

---

NEED TRAINING?

Frank Massey runs regular courses at his well-equipped Preston workshop; everything from basic engine management introductions to full-blown, 'hands on', system-specific tuition.
Call 01772 201597 for details.

---

costly and tricky to put right. Many traditional fuel injection specialists will not touch diesel cars for this very reason.

William advises that it's vital to categorise the type of fault first – be it mechanical or electrical. All the basics have to be checked such as whether there is air in the fuel, if the supply is good, if the filters are blocked etc. Then, having established that all is well, you must switch to an electronic diagnostic approach using code readers, breakout boxes and oscilloscopes. The cost of the parts means that guessing really isn't a viable option with these systems. If you decide the pump is faulty, for example, it's not simply a matter of paying the high price of the part – fitting and setting up requires special timing equipment and plenty of experience.

PREPARATION

With this TDi engine one of the most important factors for good, reliable running (as with any diesel) is that the quality of the fuel remains good. It is important that the air filter is kept clear of obstructions and that the fuel filters are changed regularly, in accordance with the service schedule.

Remember that any reduction in fuel supply, or a hole in the pipework which allows air to enter the system, will lead directly to drivability problems. Although this is strictly a mechanical problem, it can easily be wrongly diagnosed as a serious problem with the pump.

Check the quality and integrity of all the connections and inspect the ECU for signs of water damage. There is a splash guard fitted as standard, but sometimes this may go missing and problems will almost certainly result. William has come across ECUs which have been rusted to the mounting on which they sit!

Any normal diesel engine will sweat

No 3 cylinder injector contains needle lift sensor.

54

ELECTRONIC DIAGNOSTICS!

oil to some extent but this 1.9-litre unit is no worse than any other. Ideally, the engine should be kept reasonably clean but, if you choose steam cleaning for this, take care.

Be particularly on your guard if you know the car has undergone any major mechanical repair work. William came across an example on which the gearbox had been changed. Unfortunately, a careless technician had managed to pinch some of the wiring loom between the gearbox and the bell housing and this had shorted out the ECU. The luckless garage replaced the damaged ECU with a brand new one and, of course, exactly the same thing happened again! At this point they decided to check properly for the cause and eventually then found the pinched wires. A lesson to us all I think!

On this application, most of the wiring is covered in a canvass-like insulated wrapping and this can have a tendency to rot. Check for this carefully as electrical shorts will wreak havoc!

DIESEL DOWNFALLS

Despite being generally reliable, this 1.9 VW engine does have its share of characteristic weaknesses. First, and probably the most common among these is a problem which relates to the needle lift sensor.

This is built into injector number three and its role is to inform the ECU about engine stroke for ignition timing purposes. A small rod is moved within a coil to generate a voltage that can be interpreted by the ECU. The problem is that with age the injector needle becomes inefficient and eventually fails to operate. The upshot is that, although the engine will normally still run, power and top speed performance are noticeably reduced, and the dash light (glowplug light!) is triggered too.

William believes that part of the problem stems from the type of diesel we use here in the UK. The high levels of sulphur contained within the fuel have a detrimental effect on its lubricating ability, and this can be costly for both the main injection pump and the injectors. Generally, the system is pretty resistant to injector deteriora-

Coolant temperature sensor (NTC) for engine management.

tion, apart from in the case of No 3! Once the operation of this one starts to become sluggish, then the signal sent from the lift sensor to the ECU is affected and the system goes down hill rapidly.

Putting the condition right essentially means replacing No 3 injector. Unfortunately, this injector and its associated sensor take the form of a single, sealed unit and so have to be replaced as one component, costing about £280. This then throws up the dilemma of whether or not to replace the other three remaining injectors at the same time – might they all be similarly bad? On the basis of good workshop practice it would seem sensible to do so but, of course, there is the cost factor to be considered.

William tends to opt for a compromise here. His suggestion is that the No 3 injector should be renew, but that the other three should be removed and mechanically tested for flow rates, spray pattern and the presence of 'dribbling'. The conventional injectors can be refurbished if problems are found, and this will save some money.

With this problem in mind, William

advises owners always to use the highest quality fuel they can find. It may also be advisable to employ a diesel conditioning treatment at regular intervals to help lubricate the pump and injectors.

Unfortunately, this type of injector problem can occur at any time. There seems to be no predictability about the condition, and William has seen cases on cars which have covered just 30,000, while on others it might not happen for the first 100,000 miles.

Another relatively common failure on this Golf diesel application is caused by problems with the crank angle sensor. Root causes can be poor electrical connections, water ingress or dirt contamination – or a combination of all three! The sensor's location, at the bottom of the bell housing, makes it vulnerable to attack from all the usual undesirables. It can also be damaged by ham-fisted mechanics changing starter motors or clutches. This sensor is of the magnetic type and takes its input from four points on the flywheel, each of which denotes a cylinder.

Any problem with this sensor will throw the management system into 'limp home' mode so performance will be noticeably inhibited and the glowplug light on the dash will shine at all times. Owners may also notice a reluctance for the engine to start and increased smoke from the exhaust when it eventually does. This will often be grey in colour, indicating that the timing is incorrect. Always check the connections first, because this is the simplest thing to put right. If these are OK, then the output must be checked using an oscilloscope and, if a problem is found, replacement is the only solution. New crank angle sensors cost a more reasonable £90 or so, according to William, and fitting is a simple operation.

The third fault we've selected

TECHNICAL SPECIFICATIONS

Component	Voltage output	ECM pin
Air mass meter	1V at 950rpm 4V at 3,000rpm	P13
Coolant temperature sensor	4V @ 20°C 1.5V hot	P14
Air temperature sensor	3.8V cold 1.7V warm	P64
Crank angle sensor	Digital, 14V peak-to-peak at idle, A/C	P8
Fuel quantity sensor	Digital 12V square wave	P30
Fuel temperature sensor	5V cold 4.2V hot	P63
Main relay	0.8V ign. on 12.4V ign. off	P42
Battery ignition control	–	P38
EGR solenoid	Square wave varying duty cycle	P25
Trigger for Injection valve	–	P51
Glow plug relay	–	P6

VW GOLF 1.9 TDi

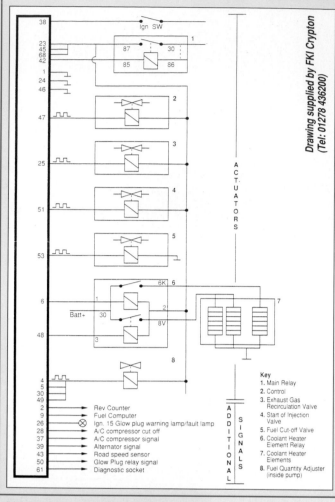

Drawing supplied by FKI Crypton (Tel: 01278 436200)

A
C
T
U
A
T
O
R
S

Ign SW

Batt+

6K
8V

Key
1. Main Relay
2. Control
3. Exhaust Gas Recirculation Valve
4. Start of Injection Valve
5. Fuel Cut-off Valve
6. Coolant Heater Element Relay
7. Coolant Heater Elements
8. Fuel Quantity Adjuster (inside pump)

A
D
D
I
T
I
O
N
A
L

S
I
G
N
A
L
S

Rev Counter
Fuel Computer
Ign. 15 Glow plug warning lamp/fault lamp
A/C compressor cut off
A/C compressor signal
Alternator signal
Road speed sensor
Glow Plug relay signal
Diagnostic socket

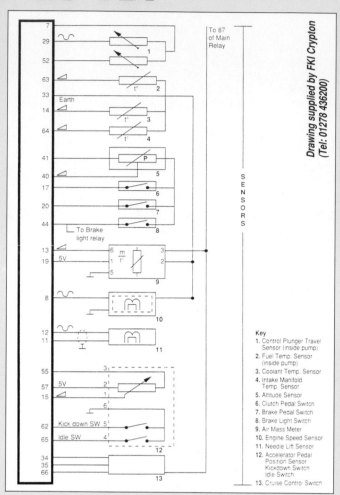

Drawing supplied by FKI Crypton (Tel: 01278 436200)

To 87 of Main Relay

Earth

To Brake light relay

5V

5V

Kick down SW
Idle SW

S
E
N
S
O
R
S

Key
1. Control Plunger Travel Sensor (inside pump)
2. Fuel Temp. Sensor (inside pump)
3. Coolant Temp. Sensor
4. Intake Manifold Temp. Sensor
5. Altitude Sensor
6. Clutch Pedal Switch
7. Brake Pedal Switch
8. Brake Light Switch
9. Air Mass Meter
10. Engine Speed Sensor
11. Needle Lift Sensor
12. Accelerator Pedal Position Sensor Kickdown Switch Idle Switch
13. Cruise Control Switch

Diagnostic socket in dash area, next to ashtray – J1692 type 16 pin.

concerns the diesel injection pump itself. This is a serious piece of kit, and not one to be meddled with by the inexperienced! It has a tendency to suffer with an internal fault, which presents itself as a deterioration in top speed performance – the car simply gets slow. What actually happens inside, according to William, is that a problem develops with the control mechanism for the governor. The up-

shot is that maximum revs cannot be obtained and so top-end performance suffers.

Unfortunately, the pump is not sensed by the management system, and so no light on the dash is triggered when such a problem occurs. To complicate matters further, William says that this trouble cannot be detected diagnostically either. Replacement of the pump is the only solution but, with this costing anything from £1,500 to £2,000, it is vital to be sure about your diagnosis before taking the plunge!

In practice, this complaint can be mistaken for a slack throttle cable except, of course, this car does not have one! As already mentioned, this car runs a 'fly-by-wire' throttle system, with no cable at all. The throttle pedal has an idle switch built in, which acts to reduce fuel flow to the pump as the throttle is released. Also, there is a 'kick-down' switch to tell the ECU when the pedal has been floored, so that more fuel can be supplied to meet the increased demand effectively. By and large, this state-of-the-art system is proving reliable so far.

One other problem which William has encountered concerns the brake pedal switch. The ECU uses inputs

from this to activate the fuel cut-off mechanism so that diesel is not wasted during braking. It is important that this switch is correctly set up, otherwise fuel cut-off can be activated at the wrong time and the engine may begin to stall under braking. The switch may also become faulty with the effect that fuel cut-off is being activated at random.

The setting-up procedure is detailed in the workshop manual, but is based essentially around pedal travel. William says that a VAG service tool is required for this important job, unless you are expert with a breakout box and have the relevant data relating to correct switch output etc.

He adds, as a final point, that it is important to monitor the voltage output of the air mass meter. This is a critical factor on this system. The meter is based around a hot wire, which is cooled as the induction air is drawn across it. It is a sensitive component and is easily damaged so take great care if you have to remove it. As with most other components on this engine, replacements are expensive!

NEXT MONTH
Ford Mondeo 1.8TD.

ELECTRONIC DIAGNOSTICS!

Tracing and fixing faults in electronic engine management systems

Number 52: *Ford's Mondeo oil-burner is a popular and reliable option for those seeking the economic benefits of running a diesel. But is its engine management bullet-proof too? Chris Graham finds out.*

Continuing with the diesel theme, we are featuring a Mondeo 1.8 TD this month. The engine is a trusty old cast iron unit, which has already enjoyed lengthy service on Ford Escort and Fiesta diesel applications over the years.

In this guise it's fitted with a tur-bocharger, intercooler and electronic engine management and, as far as we know, there are no plans for a re-placement engine just yet (new direct injection model, due out next year – sub-Ed). For some well-informed and expert technical comment on this motor, I returned to bonny Scotland where independent diagnostic special-ist William McLaren (Tel: 0370 737257) waited to tell all over that tra-

TURBO INTERCOOLER

EGR SOLENOID

ADVANCE SOLENOID

AIR MASS METER – HOT WIRE TYPE

THROTTLE POT ON LEVER

COOLANT TEMPERATURE SENSOR (*UNDER THERMOSTAT HOUSING*)

CVT – CURRENT TO VACUUM TRANSDUCER

ENGINE MANAGEMENT

The ECU used on this 1.8 TD has 28 pins and runs a system called Ford EDC (Electronic Diesel Control). Later applications, from 1996 onwards, have a much larger control unit with 104 pins and a newer software package which, William says, is similar to the EECV system used on the latest petrol-engined Fords.

There is a 16-pin OBD (on board diagnostics) socket located under the steering column, which is used to access fault codes. Unfortunately, there is no light on the dashboard to warn of engine management faults so these can go unnoticed. William believes there are about 18 fault codes listed, which is not particularly comprehensive.

The primary triggers for this system are supplied to the ECU by the crankshaft position sensor, which monitors engine speed during cranking and at all other times, and the coolant temperature sensor. The latter is required because there is a cold advance solenoid (located on the pump) which works rather like a mechanical choke but is controlled electronically.

If this is not functioning as it should then starting problems will be encountered because fuelling will be wrong. A failure of crankshaft sensor output will prevent the engine from running too.

Elsewhere in the system there is a throttle potentiometer, which is mounted on top of the pump at the front of the engine. This informs the ECU of throttle position and is supplied with a five-volt reference. An air mass meter is used to measure the quantity of air being drawn into the engine, allowing the ECU to calculate correct pump timing.

On the emission control side of things there is an EGR solenoid and valve. This introduces some of the exhaust gas back into the inlet manifold to cool combustion process and thus reduce emission levels.

William adds that the EGR valve sometimes will stick, and that this can be highlighted by excessive smoking from the exhaust during acceleration. A sticking valve can also result in poor general performance if the exhaust gases are being fed back into the system constantly without ECU control.

Fuel injection timing is controlled by the pump and this must be set correctly. The ECU has the ability to adjust timing, but only marginally, so initial pump set-up is a vital factor. Problems with the pump do occur, often resulting from abuse. Replacements cost about £500.

---

ditional Scottish delicacy – a McDonalds Quarterpounder with cheese!

The engine is a reliable one and generally durable. It will suffer, of course, if neglected. Timing belt failure is disastrous, and can be regarded as a virtual certainty if change intervals are ignored. There can also be problems with the timing belt idlers, which have been modified from plastic to steel on later applications. The non-metal versions were apparently not up to the job, hence the specification change.

Electronically, the system is relatively reliable too. There are some characteristic failings, many of which relate to the quality of installation. William believes this could be better, particularly as far as the location of the ECU is concerned. It's unprotected

NEED TRAINING?
Frank Massey runs regular courses at his well-equipped Preston workshop; everything from basic engine management introductions to full-blown, 'hands on', system-specific tuition.
Call 01772 201597 for details.

position behind the offside headlight means it's vulnerable to water ingress – not a particularly good start!

PREPARATION

Before starting work on this engine, the wise technician will always cast a critical eye over the whole under-bonnet installation. Check for obvious defects such as broken, disconnected or chafed vacuum pipes. Check especially those running to the EGR valve and the turbo wastegate (the turbo is found beneath the intercooler). Check also for splits in the trunking running between the air mass meter and the inlet manifold.

Pay attention also to all electrical connections, looking particularly for signs of corrosion and poor fitting connectors. The wiring leading to the throttle potentiometer can be prone to chafing on nearby brackets if the component has been fiddled with – which is all too often the case.

Another potential black spot is the point at which the crank angle sensor's wire passes the starter motor. Sometimes it can get pinched between the starter and the engine block. Also take the trouble to remove and check the ECU carefully for signs of corrosion. Assuming the ignition is switched off, then William says there is no risk attached to unplugging the control unit. Look for any marks on the casing which might suggest water ingress.

The box cannot be opened, but if problems with water are evident then he advises that action be taken to protect the unit by bagging it and its connector. The danger, of course, is that

The throttle potentiometer is a favourite for fiddling – check the condition of its wiring carefully.

ELECTRONIC DIAGNOSTICS!

condensation build-up may lead to additional trouble but this is perhaps the lesser of two evils. At least if you are aware of the problem, regular checks can be made.

MONDEO MALADIES!

Perhaps the most common problem to afflict this Mondeo diesel application relates to the throttle potentiometer. Unfortunately, this important component is conveniently placed on top of the injection pump and presents an easy and tempting target for those who like to fiddle!

Trouble can strike with the component itself or with its wiring. Voltage output is critical and any deviations will lead to driveability problems. There will be noticeable hesitation right across the rev range and engine idle speed may well be lower than normal. From new the unit is sealed with blue paint but, according to William, many people find this irresistible and feel duty bound to 'dive in'!

The idle speed is set by the base voltage output from the throttle pot, so if this is upset, then things will never be right. There are mechanical stops which must be checked to ensure that the lever is correctly set when at rest.

The problem here, for the inexperienced, is that specialist knowledge and tooling is required. If you don't have access to the right data, with regard to voltage outputs, then you are in trouble. And, as we've said so many times in this series already, good quality, accurate data is the key to successful diagnostics.

William says that a Ford service tool is needed to set the base position and that this must correspond with the appropriate voltage output. If you have no voltage data then the only option is to take readings, using a multimeter, from another car which is known to be correct. Once the pot has been set correctly, then output should remain correct right across the range from there.

Inept fiddling with the throttle pot can also put its wiring in jeopardy. The big danger is that upsetting the component will lower its wiring so that it comes into contact with the throttle lever beneath. This will inevitably lead to chafing and po-

The ECU is prone to water ingress. The condition of its connector can suffer too.

tential electrical shorting that will send spurious output readings to the ECU, causing hesitation.

Spotting this problem requires careful inspection as the damaged side of the wire will be hidden from view. The sensible solution is to tape up any stripped areas carefully and then to use a cable tie to secure the wires to the bracket or the pump so that they are out of harms way.

If the potentiometer itself is damaged, and this does happen, then replacement is the only answer. You will be able to tell if this is the case, because it will be impossible to achieve the correct voltage output – its tolerance will have drifted out of specification.

The pot is based around a variable

resistor track and this can either be damaged by careless probing, or by contamination. The unit is a throwaway item once damaged and William says that replacements cost about £40.

Another common trouble spot is the crank angle sensor. Its location is at that heart of the problem, but age can play a part too. It's found at a very low point within the bell housing and can be damaged mechanically by careless vehicle jacking or even by impact damage from stones. The chances of problems are greatly increased if the factory-fit plastic undershield is missing. William says it's relatively common for this not to be replaced after servicing, so be warned. Not only does such neglect expose the sensor to the risk of being struck, but it also greatly speeds the corrosive process.

The symptoms of crank angle sensor failure are not hard to spot – the engine will not run! However, leading up to this the owner may well have noticed an increased reluctance for the engine to start. Obviously you will have to isolate the problem, making sure there is fuel being supplied to the pump and injectors. The crank angle sensor, which is a simple magnetic device and takes its input from the flywheel, is a 'sensed' component, so when a fault is detected by the ECU it, in turn, closes down the cold start advance device.

Testing for sensor failure ideally requires the services of an oscilloscope, although William adds that it is possible to make a meaningful diagnosis using a multimeter set on AC range. Obviously it is essential to test for continuity in the supply wires, and if this exists, but there is no output, then the sensor is at fault.

Replacement is the only option because repairs are not possible. The sensor is a straightforward screw fit and a new one will cost you about £27.

Finally, while by no means a stunning performer, this Mondeo diesel should normally be a willing worker, and any noticeable deterioration in performance can point to a problem with the air mass meter. The difficulty here is that there are other possible causes too, so careful interrogation and a methodical approach are required before launching into a process of component replacement.

William's chosen method of diagnosis involves first checking the output of the air mass meter, which is of the 'hot wire' variety. Ideally, he would use an oscilloscope to check not only the value of this output, but its quality as

TECHNICAL SPECIFICATIONS

Coolant temp sensor	P26-P27	3.4V cold (10°C) 0.6V hot (90°C)
Throttle pot	P27-P21 P27-A8	5V supply from ECU 0.6-0.8V at idle 4.7V WOT
Crank sensor	P22-P23	8V AC signal at idle
Cold advance solenoid	P3	Earth control via ECU until engine reaches working temp.
Light load solenoid	P4	Digital signal calculated by coolant temp. sensor. Throttle pot position and ECU control vary dwell control signal.
Air mass meter	P6	1.0V output at 850rpm

Additional pin terminations:
P1/P13 – Air con (if fitted)
P2 – Earth control cold advance relay
P8/P17/P20 – Diagnostic socket
P10 – Positive battery ignition control

The diagnostic socket is found inside the car, behind a hinged cover on the underside of the column.

FORD EDC

BATTERY (-)

A/C RELAY

AIR MASS
METER
CONNECTIONS

DIESEL PUMP
UNIT

15

BATTERY (+)   + BAT IGN CTRL

FUSE F9
20A

FUSE F4
20A

30

85   86

87

COLD ADVANCE SOLENOID

CSS

TPS

DIAGNOSTIC SKT

CTS

EGR VALVE EARTH CTRL

well. The engine needs to be running and held at various rev settings so that voltage outputs can be monitored across the range.

Once again, the whole business hinges on you having access to accurate data relating to correct component output. The tolerance on air mass meter output is relatively small, so slight variations can throw everything out of specification.

If this is the case then, unfortunately, there is no remedial action to be taken. The component is unserviceable and must be replaced, at a cost probably in excess of £250. The hot wire operates a regular 'burn off' function and if this fails, then the wire becomes contaminated and its effective-

ness is lost.

However, if the voltage outputs are found to be correct, William's advice is to check for problems on the fuel

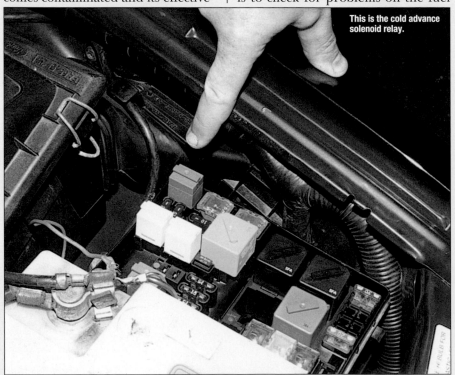

This is the cold advance solenoid relay.

side, in particular vacuum leaks. Air leaks are commonly caused by problems with the hand priming unit. This is a device intended for use when changing the fuel filter as part of the routine servicing procedure. It contains a rubber diaphragm, which perishes with age.

The air leaks which result can create early morning starting problems – the fuel is allowed to drain back into the tank overnight, requiring excessive engine cranking in the morning to replenish the supply. This condition can be mistaken for crank angle sensor failure.

Also, any air allowed into the system will degrade the fuel and reduce the effectiveness of the pump's operation. This will also lead to poor performance and often an erratic idle. The primer has to be replaced as a complete unit and will cost £85 or so. William says two different primers are used, which one your vehicle requires depends on its age.

NEXT MONTH
Mercedes-Benz 190E.

ELECTRONIC DIAGNOSTICS!

Tracing and fixing faults in electronic engine management systems

Number 53: *The seemingly ever-reliable and constantly desirable Mercedes-Benz 190E gets the treatment this month. Chris Graham tells the story.*

The Mercedes-Benz 190E is neat, functional and reliable. It's a typically German car in many respects and one which justifies its reputation of being a thoroughly good motor car. But what of the problems? There must be some, surely?

Well, of course there are, and to find out more I made a welcome return to

TYPICAL FAULTS
1. **Injection quality**
2. **Fuel pressure**
3. **Poor starting**

Preston where, at Fuel Injection Services (Tel: 01772 201597) proprietor Frank Massey waited with the answers. The 190 comes with a variety of engine

sizes, but by far the most popular is the 2.0-litre variant.

This engine employs the tried and trusted Bosch KE Jetronic fuel control system, and couples it with a separate ignition module to monitor the sparks.

The KE system was developed from the original K Jetronic, with the K standing for 'constant' in German. The

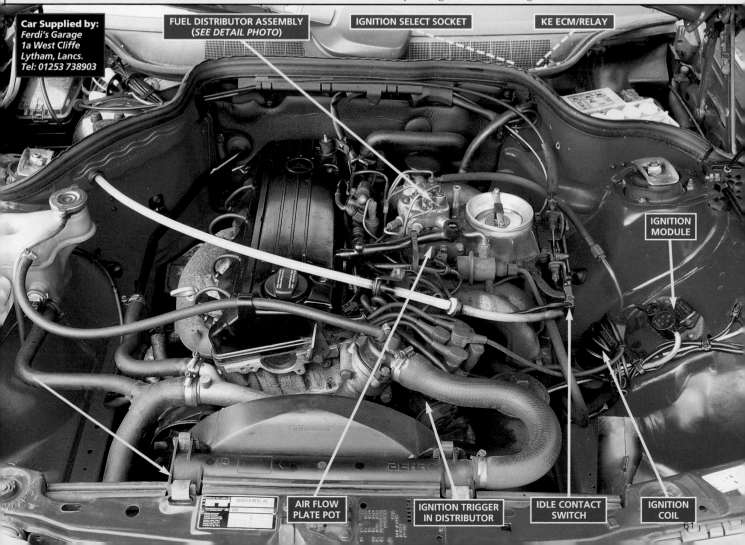

Car Supplied by:
Ferdi's Garage
1a West Cliffe
Lytham, Lancs.
Tel: 01253 738903

FUEL DISTRIBUTOR ASSEMBLY *(SEE DETAIL PHOTO)*

IGNITION SELECT SOCKET

KE ECM/RELAY

IGNITION MODULE

AIR FLOW PLATE POT

IGNITION TRIGGER IN DISTRIBUTOR

IDLE CONTACT SWITCH

IGNITION COIL

ENGINE MANAGEMENT

There are two very obvious and totally separate aspects to this system. One is the mechanical function of the fuel control and the other is the electronic over-ride. Although separate entities, both work in tandem and their inter-relationship must be understood and appreciated.

Looking at the mechanical side first, the fuel tank is fitted with an externally mounted, gravity-fed fuel pump. This is a high pressure unit capable of achieving up to 10 bar (150psi or so) on a default test when the outlets are shut off. The fuel is passed through a high pressure filter and on to the fuel delivery head, from where the fuel is piped to the individual injectors.

The delivery head, found beneath the air cleaner housing, incorporates an air flow plate – a round disc that is opened and closed by the varying passage of air being drawn into the engine.

This is a purely mechanical device and the amount of its deflection acts, via a connection beam, upon a fuel plunger in the centre of the fuel distributor. The movement ratio of this beam is 14.7:1, which is the air/fuel ratio. So this ensures that the fuel/air mixture is always maintained correctly.

There is obviously a need for cold start enrichment, acceleration enrichment and over-fuel cut-off. These are the functions which the electronics side of the system takes care of. All are achieved by a variable damping effect on the flow plate, which is altered accordingly. For example, the greater the damping, the less the plate will rise and so fuel supply will be reduced.

Because the fuel system is operated at high pressure, you are looking at a delivery rate of 90 litres an hour or more, which is more or less double a conventional electrical system. There are four mechanical injectors which are pressure-operated too. The car we looked at was fitted with a temperature-sensitive auxiliary air valve and a pressure regulator, which takes the form of a diaphragm on the outlet side of the fuel circuit.

You may also find some 190s fitted with a fuel accumulator, mounted near the fuel pump. This is a storage reservoir with a spring-loaded diaphragm, which, when the engine is switched off and the pump stops running, maintains some pressure in the system so that fuel is instantly available for the injectors upon restart. To achieve this there are two important one-way valves – one in the pump and the other in the fuel pressure regulator. These allow what's know as 'decay' pressure to be maintained by the accumulator.

On the electrical side there is a separate set of important components. Mounted on the side of the fuel delivery head is the business end of the electronic control system – the electronic actuator. This is basically an electro-magnetic switch which uses current passing between two separate armatures to control a valve. It is operated at very high speed and considerable accuracy, to vary the pressure of the fuel being supplied to the delivery head. It can be closed completely to provide over-run fuel cut off, and can also be used to richen the mixture for cold start operations and acceleration.

Elsewhere there is a relatively simple 25-pin ECU tucked away at the back of the engine bay on the n/s bulkhead. Only about half the pins will be wired up, but the terminations do vary from model to model as the system was evolved. Also there is a coolant sensor; a thermo time switch; a cold start valve (usually); an extra, electronic injector, which is driven only during cranking for a limited period, when the ambient temperature falls below a predetermined figure – as dictated by the thermo-time switch.

There is an idle switch and a full-throttle switch, to indicate when over-run fuel cut-off and acceleration enrichment respectively are required; an ignition control module and a potentiometer, which produces a variable voltage by measuring the degree to which the air flow plate support beam rotates on its pivot.

A composite relay is found close to the ECU and you will also often find a separate relay next to the ECU, which is fitted with a simple fuse on top – in fact this is the main control fuse.

In cases when Lambda control is fitted (on late versions), an oxygen sensor feeds an input into the ECU, which then controls the current to the fuel control actuator.

Basic fuel mixture control is achieved mechanically using a simple screw with a 3mm hex drive socket, directly in the middle of the air flow plate body. Interestingly, even on the closed loop control versions, the mixture can be set to achieve the best Lambda switch – a unique feature because a normal closed loop system has no adjustment potential at all.

There is no dashboard warning light to indicate problems, and no code reading facility whatsoever. But since there are no complex electrical signals involved, a decent multimeter and a quality pressure gauge are about all you need.

significance of this is that the fuel injectors are open permanently and operate by a high speed 'chattering' action rather than a complete open/close cycle.

The addition of the letter 'E' heralded the introduction of some degree of electronic over-ride, replacing the older mechanical/hydraulic system. Hydraulic control pressures are still used by KE, but these are now controlled electronically.

Overall, Frank is a real fan of this system. He describes it as virtually bomb-proof and, coming from him, that's a compliment! The only two things it does not like are water and grit. Get either or both mixed in with the fuel and you will have big problems. The installation is good too. Very neat and capable of high quality performance. When set up properly with premium injectors, you can achieve fu-

elling which is every bit as good as the latest, most complex systems around currently. Technically it is a very good system – the proof of this being the fact that the mighty Mercedes-Benz stuck with its relative simplicity for so long.

PREPARATION

This car's reputation for reliability is a good one, and deservedly so according to Frank. Nevertheless, there are still factors to be checked, the first of which being the distributor cap. As standard these are fitted with a black plastic cover which is 'riveted' into place by tiny straps under the cap. Frank's advice is to use a junior hacksaw to cut through these so that the cover can be removed.

Often this cover will trap dirt and debris beneath it and so the cap itself becomes contaminated, leading to the risk of electrical tracking and a reduction in efficiency. Remove the cap and wash it thoroughly, inside and out. Replace it with a genuine Bosch component if in any doubt about condition, if not dry completely and replace.

The rotor arm usually endures a hard

life. The burn time, uniquely on Mercedes-Benz, is about 2.5ms, which is a full millisecond longer than most other applications. For this reason the tip of the arm tends to become eroded and should be inspected. Clean it up carefully with a file or, better still, replace with a new one if wear is very evident.

The plug leads suffer at the plug end. They feature a metallic shroud which serves a couple of specific purposes. First, it protects against exces-

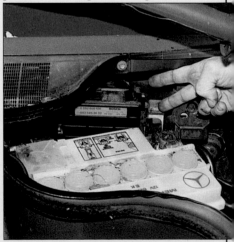

Here is the ECU and, to the right, the main control fuse on top of its single relay.

ELECTRONIC DIAGNOSTICS!

sive heat but it also shields against RF to prevent HT 'spikes' breaking free. With age the leads can suffer from electrical tracking. The plug voltage is allowed to find a path back to earth via the lead, which causes misfires and poor running. The problem is usually caused by a build-up of conductive debris on the inside of the shrouds, which, combined with deteriorating rubber condition, allows voltage to drain away.

The big give-away of this condition is a brown 'corona' stain effect around the base of the ceramic plug body. This proves the point without doubt. If you spot it then replace the original wire cored leads with more modern carbon alternatives. Frank also tends to favour BMW plug connectors, as a more durable upgrade.

Remove the air cleaner to gain access to the fuel delivery head and air flow plate. The plate will, in most cases, be showing signs of oily deposits and these should be carefully washed off. Check in detail for signs of damage or pitting around the edge of the plate. There is a tiny gap between the plate and the body, and this is adjustable. If you notice that the plate is off centre, or fouling on its travel, this must be sorted out to re-establish unhindered movement.

Wash around plug apertures with carburettor cleaner, refit plugs and leads and then check the throttle linkage. This features a fairly complicated cam arrangement for movement transfer, and can suffer with dirt ingress. Wash and check all the small rollers for smooth operation, then lightly lubricate. There are two return springs in this system and it is vital that both are fitted and working.

SORTING OUT TROUBLE

The 190E is, by and large, an extremely reliable car. Problems, when they do occur, tend to stem from age-related defects rather than inherent trouble. The first and most common of these relates to fuelling, and is caused by a deterioration of injection quality.

The symptoms of this may well be higher than normal exhaust emissions (mainly HC) and a reluctance for the engine to idle smoothly unless the mix-

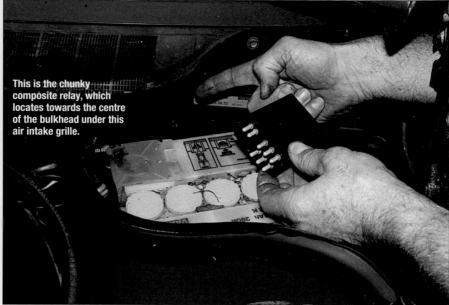

This is the chunky composite relay, which locates towards the centre of the bulkhead under this air intake grille.

ture is set richer. You may have to run it at 1-1.5% CO to achieve a smooth tickover.

At the root of all this is injector performance. Carbon build up on and around the injector head prevents effective atomisation, so efficiency is reduced. Frank says that many years ago he took the decision to stop trying to refurbish KE injectors simply because to clean them effectively is difficult.

Because they are mechanical injectors they cannot be driven and so clearing the head of contaminant build up can be a problem. The return spring on the pintel will not be shifted until fluid pressure reaches about 3.6 bar. This is not possible using conventional ultrasonic injector cleaning equipment.

By far the best solution is to specify new injectors. Frank advises fitting Bosch units only. Price may vary with the most expensive being around £40 but, considering a quality component will run for anything up to 80,000

miles (assuming an absence of grit and dirt), they are not bad value for money. Choose later spec injectors when you can – the latest brass-bodied ones are the best. Always remember that the business end of fuel delivery is the injector. If in doubt take them to a specialist for flow bench testing before opting to replace.

A sensible additional measure is also to change the fuel filter. As Frank says, there is no point in fitting new parts to a system which is going to continue passing dirt. Once again, opt for the genuine replacement. Bosch units include a water membrane which is important.

If you do change the injectors, the fuelling mixture will have to be re-calibrated. If a fuelling problem remains then you must move on to the next stage which relates to incorrect fuel pressure.

If you come across a problem with mixture control when the engine is hot then a pressure problem could be the cause. Fuel pressure is controlled by two aspects – mechanical and electrical. There is a very simple way of determining into which area the problem falls. To establish whether a fuelling fault relates to a mechanical or an electrical (KE) problem, unplug the two-pin socket from the hydraulic control actuator to remove all KE control functions.

If then the mixture becomes right (normally faults send it rich), then the problem is obviously electronic in nature. If the problem persists with the KE disconnected, then you must put gauges on to check system and control pressures.

Electronic problems will almost always stem from a defect

TECHNICAL SPECIFICATIONS

Component/function	Technical data
Temperature sensor	Cold – 2.5-2.8V Hot – 0.5-0.8V
Idle control valve	Digital output, 12V to ground (if fitted)
Actuator current	Cold – 11-15MA Hot – 0MA Snap – 715MA
Air flow pot.	Output pulsed, 0.25-0.5V to 4.5V with open throttle, Over-run cut-off 60MA
Fuel pump current	6-8A
Fuel flow rate	Minimum 70 lt/hr Maximum 110 lt/hr
Fuel injector opening pressure	3.6-4.0 bar
Emissions	Idle – CO 1%, HC 100-300ppm Cruise – CO 0.5%, HC 50-100ppm

BOSCH KE JETRONIC

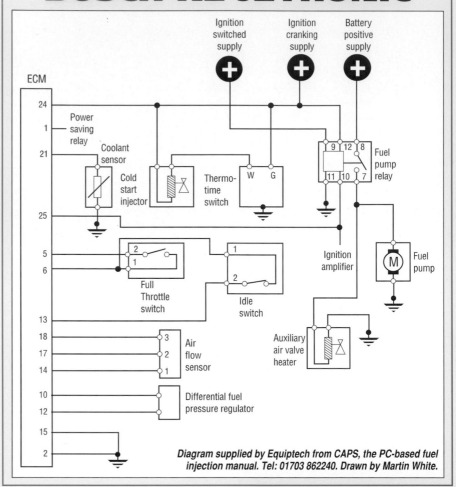

Diagram supplied by Equiptech from CAPS, the PC-based fuel injection manual. Tel: 01703 862240. Drawn by Martin White.

with the coolant sensor – it's usually found to be outputting the wrong value. To check the electrical inputs to the actuator, voltage measurement is not really good enough because it is a current-controlled device. Frank's suggested method for doing this it to attach a fuel pressure gauge and check for correct pressures when the engine is both cold and hot.

If you establish that the problem is, in fact, mechanical in nature, then the cause could well lie with the fuel delivery head. There are only two solutions to this – buy a new one for about £400, or have the original re-calibrated. The latter is a very specialised business and should only be entrusted to an experienced expert. Seek advice from a specialist like Frank about placing this sort of work.

Re-calibration costs about half the price of replacement. Defects within the delivery head, such as conditions which deliver more fuel to just one injector, for example, can be corrected by re-calibration.

The final problem we'll deal with here concerns poor starting. Sometimes a car might prove temperamental to start from cold. It will idle badly, will prove reluctant to rev and will be generally flat until the engine is warm, at which point performance returns to

Metal ends to original plug leads will cause problems with age.

normal. The good news with this system is that if you unplug the ECU, the engine will run totally as a mechanical system but without cold start, fuel cut-off or acceleration enrichment – hence the good hot engine performance.

Poor cold start performance is usually caused by the control fuse blowing, which prevents the KE system from powering up. Alternatively, the same symptoms could relate to a coolant sensor/sensor wiring failure. This tends to be an age-related fault. Either way, rectification is a simple matter of component replacement.

NEXT MONTH
Ford ESC ignition.

FUEL ADJUST PORT · AIR FLOW PLATE · FUEL DISTRIBUTOR · ELECTRONIC ACTIVATOR · BY-PASS AIR BLEED · COLD START INJECTOR · SYSTEM PRESSURE REGULATOR

ELECTRONIC DIAGNOSTICS!

Tracing and fixing faults in electronic engine management systems

Number 54: Chris Graham gets back to basics with a look at the simple but very effective electronic ignition system used by Ford on their late carburettor-equipped models.

This month we are departing from the usual format and concentrating on the 'stand alone' ignition system used by Ford on a number of their popular, small-engined vehicle applications.

Commonly referred to as Ford ESC (Electronic Spark Control), this system is officially denoted as Ford UPAC –

TYPICAL FAULTS
1. **Crank angle sensor**
2. **Earth points**
3. **Engine stalling**

these letters making reference to the presence of an air temperature sensor within the system. It should be noted here that there is a very similar, but

crucially different system, called ESC H2, which Ford also used. This relies on a larger 22-pin control unit so the difference between this and the smaller 12-pin unit used by ESC should be obvious.

Frank Massey, proprietor of Preston-based Fuel Injection Services (Tel: 01772 201597) explains that

THERMO SWITCH
FOR RADIATOR FAN

ESC
MODULE

TEMPERATURE
GAUGE SENSOR

COOLANT SENSOR FOR ESC
(UNDER MANIFOLD)

CRANK ANGLE SENSOR
(REAR BLOCK)

VACUUM
HOSE

IGNITION MANAGEMENT

The control module which regulates this Ford system makes use of a vacuum device to determine engine load. There is also a coil pack which is, in effect, two coils in one unit, with each end of each coil firing a single plug.

Ford used this electronic spark control system for several years in varying guises. The very early versions were seen on 1.8-litre Sierras and the controller in those days was a relatively large one (normal ECU size). The development of electronic technology meant that the size was reduced and the unit featured here is not much bigger than a cigarette packet.

The system itself is very simple. Electronics are kept to a minimum and the carburettor has no sophisticated control features apart from, in some cases, an electronic fuel cut-off valve on certain applications. This is not present on Frank's car but he says that it is a simple solenoid which closes when the ignition is switched off, to shut off the idle duct.

Other significant components include a crank angle sensor, a coolant sensor, an air temperature sensor, an internal MAP sensor within the control unit – supplied by a rubber pipe running into the inlet manifold.

There is no distributor cap, rotor arm or coil king lead to worry about. Overall quality is excellent and problems, if they do occur, will often be caused by external factors such as careless repair work or water ingress.

There is no potential on this system for code reading, not that it is really needed anyway. A multimeter can be used to good effect for basic tests (electrical supplies, dwell and voltage drop etc). However, assessing crank angle sensor performance requires an oscilloscope. This is a complex signal, running at a reasonably high frequency, which can only be interrogated once the waveform has been displayed.

Spark voltage can only be measured using an inductive pick-up, which points you in the direction of dedicated tuning equipment designed for use on DIS systems. Alternatively, experienced operators can make use of inductive pick-ups, which can be linked to a lab oscilloscope or in coil primary circuits.

Ford ESC is a simple 'wasted spark' ignition system, which makes use of speed, load and temperature inputs that are processed by a separate control module.

It was launched in 1989, ran through until 1993, and is found on the 'bread and butter' Ford models which utilised the old carburettor-equipped pushrod engine. These include Fiesta 1.0, 1.1 and 1.3-litre applications, and the Escort 1.1 and 1.3-litre versions.

After 1993 Ford switched to a modern single-point engine management system on these lower-end models, based on EEC IV. There remains some similarity in the ignition control functions, but this is as far as the likeness goes.

The good news, from a reliability point of view, is that basically this system is excellent. While Frank admits that it does suffer from a few characteristic niggles, overall serious failures are rare. He cannot recall actually having to change a faulty ESC module, and this is after working on literally hundreds of examples over the years.

He adds that the coil packs do have some reputation for failure but, again, he has not experienced this first hand. Remember, this is an engine which is prone to oil consumption and leaky rocker covers. Seeping oil might find its way into sensitive areas, leading to problems, but these are not the fault of the system itself.

The vehicle pictured here is Frank's own 1.3-litre Escort van, which is standard apart from a performance air filter.

PREPARATION

There is plenty of room under the bonnets of these small Fords so maintenance/tuning work is made easy. With regard to basic preparation, your first job should be to inspect the rubber MAP sensor vacuum pipe.

This is reasonably long by modern standards and, although it is supported by a clip on the hydraulic line from the brake servo, there will usually be a couple of droops along its length. For this reason it can (and usually does!) collect oil and maybe even petrol inside. Liquid sits at the low points and provides an undesirable damping effect on the air moving within.

If the pipe appears swollen at any point, fits badly at either end or is kinked along its length, then replace it. Even if the condition looks OK, it is still worth removing it and blowing it through with an air line to clear any fluid build-up within. Remember never to blow through this with it still connected to the ESC module because you will destroy the sensitive MAP sensor in a flash.

Because these engines often have a tendency to be a little smoky, the inlet manifold end of the vacuum pipe and its drilled connector, can become choked up with carbon. Any obstruction here, or elsewhere in the pipe, will affect MAP sensor operation and prevent the correct ignition point from being chosen by the control unit.

In most cases you will also find a petrol trap fitted to the vacuum pipe, which is designed to collect excess fuel. Frank is not a fan of these devices. He says that they are usually ignored and so, once full, they actually become a source of petrol. His advice is to remove it because he regards it as a needless hindrance to the passage of air. He would rather make a point of cleaning the pipe out on a regular basis, rather than relying on the trap to do the job for him.

It's also well worth having a look at the ESC module itself. This is sited in a relatively vulnerable position on the front, n/s inner wing. Road dirt and moisture can be thrown up on to this vital component, although, having said this, Frank has not come across corrosion problems. Nevertheless, it makes sense to clean away any surface dirt

Ignition contol unit is remarkably small but very effective.

ELECTRONIC DIAGNOSTICS!

and to check and lubricate the main 12-pin connector socket.

It's also good practice to remove the crank angle sensor so that it can be inspected and wiped clean as necessary. This is a magnetic component and will collect debris over the years. If you wish, the sensor can be updated with a newer version featuring gold connector pins, but Frank does not consider this really necessary.

The HT leads are usually of superb quality, assuming that cheaper pattern parts have not been fitted. The genuine Ford product is excellent in Frank's opinion, with superb rubber boots. They fit very well at the coil end and so electrical tracking is rarely a serious problem. However, do note that the coil pack is located in a potentially dirty area and oil contamination is always a risk.

If leaked oil is evident use a suitable degreaser to remove it. Steam cleaning can be effective too but, in both cases, make sure that the leads are removed and dried thoroughly before re-fitting. The coil pack itself is virtually bomb-proof as far as water ingress is concerned, but take no chances anyway and blow it off carefully with an air line.

Check the plug apertures carefully before removing the plugs. This engine can generate rust (from the cast iron cylinder head) which collects down in the plug holes. A sensible precaution is to clear as much of this away before removing the plugs because it's not the type of material you want dropping down into the cylinder bores! Always fit quality, resistive plugs and note that the correct components for this application do not have a washer – they feature a taper seat.

There can also be unwanted obstructions in the air intake system, so check the filter assembly carefully. There is also a vacuum pipe which runs from the air cleaner into the inlet manifold, and this will often be blocked.

Wash out the carburettor with a suitable cleaning fluid/spray. Oil fumes drawn in will contaminate the venturi and can also eventually block the idle jet. Remove the jet and its carrier using a 13mm spanner and clear it using the correct drill. Give it a blast of compressed air and re-fit.

The only tune-up adjustment

The coil pack is found down here at the back of the engine.

on this fixed-jet system is provided by the idle mixture control. Frank says that the ignition timing is adjustable 'electronically' using the octane adjust socket (pins 6 & 7). The connecting wires are either cut or earthed to achieve the desired effect. Consult your workshop manual for this procedure. However, the ignition can only be altered in the 'retard' direction. Frank says that the original setting is fully advanced and, in this condition, pins six and seven will be joined together and not earthed. He adds that he has never known of one that has needed to be altered from this factory setting.

Finally, bear in mind that these engines will often be noticeably 'tappety'. Don't try to cure this by setting them tight. Stick to the correct gaps (0.2-0.3mm cold) and just endure the noise or fit new cam/followers!

PROBLEM SOLVING

The first and most common problem Frank has picked-up relates to the crank angle sensor. Its signal is an AC waveform with both positive and negative values in the cycle. The signal is

slightly off-set (see diagram) by about 1.25V and features a TDC section to denote engine position.

The quality of this signal is crucial to the smooth running of the whole ignition system. An oscilloscope must be used to monitor and assess this. It provides the primary trigger into the control unit and so must be right. Debris on the sensor itself will affect this, which is why it must always be clean.

Assessing the performance of this sensor requires the use of an oscilloscope. It is unlikely that any problem will be caused by the phonic wheel, from which the sensor takes its input. In this case this is simply a series of round holes drilled in the flywheel so there is not much that can go wrong here. So trouble will be restricted to the sensor itself, or its wiring.

One of the most important factors is that the crank angle sensor's wiring should be 'screened'. The two signal wires are protected from electrical 'noise' by a shield winding around them. This protects the signals being sent from RF interference which might be picked up from the HT leads or the starter motor – the latter is located horribly close! Electrical pulsing from these sources, if allowed to interfere, will compromise the signal from the crank angle sensor.

Frank has come across several cases where this screening has not been in place and the results have been dramatic. In the worst cases the car will not run at all, or, if it does, it will appear to be over-advanced.

The only true solution is to sort out the wiring. But remember also that the starter motor may be at fault. If this is badly worn it should be changed as well, and Frank adds here the

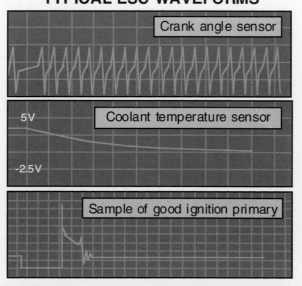

TYPICAL ESC WAVEFORMS

Crank angle sensor

5V

Coolant temperature sensor

-2.5V

Sample of good ignition primary

FORD ESC IGNITION

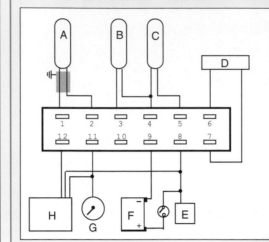

Component key:

A. Crank angle sensor
B. Air temperature sensor
C. Coolant temp. sensor
D. Octane adjust socket
E. Fuel cut-off solenoid
F. Battery
G. Rev counter
H. Coil pack

importance of specifying a quality replacement. Avoid buying cheap reconditioned units, as the quality and operational standard of these can be dubious.

Specify a new length of good quality screened cable and re-terminate it at both ends. Make sure that the screen is terminated at both ends too. Frank achieves this by cutting the insulation around the cable, soldering on a fly lead and running this directly to a good quality earth point.

The sensor itself is held in place by a 6mm screw and a ring tab terminal can be used on this as an anchorage for the screened fly lead. Frank says that such measures are rarely taken but they really do make a difference and help with the 'dumping' of any RF interference. Any decent electrical supplier will be able to provide good qual-

Coolant temperature sensor replacement is a straightforward operation.

ity, two-core screened cable.

The sensor itself can fail but replacement is both cheap and simple. There is a potential for confusion here though because two versions exist. They differ in length so you must make sure you get the one intended for carburettor-equipped cars, rather than the one intended for later fuel injected applications. The cost is about £15.

Another relatively common cause of a 'no start' condition on this vehicle is a problem with the earth points. These can become compromised, particularly with age. The reference becomes high and this prevents enough current being supplied to pull down the coil. Dwell does not take place and no spark is produced.

Dealing with these problems can be long-winded but Frank has a simple solution. Pin number nine is the main earth connection on the control unit. To solve all earthing problems cut this wire, 'solder and shrink' a fly lead to it and run this directly to the battery's negative terminal.

Also, pin four on the control unit is the earth return from the coolant temperature and air temperature sensors. Treat this in the same way. Continuing on the wiring theme, Frank has also come across problems with the loom. There is an internal connection which runs to the negative terminal on the coil pack and this can suffer from corrosion caused by water ingress as the system ages. It can create a misfire in two cylinders (half the coil) even though the coil does not appear to be faulty.

The problem is that the poor connection is not allowing a good current flow through the coil and so spark efficiency is reduced. The only solution is to cut open the loom and trace back to the faulty connection and put it right. Similar problems can affect another internal joint which supplies the

Crank angle sensor can be a cause of problems.

main ignition feed. This runs, via the main ignition switch, to the centre of the three pins on the coil and to pin eight on the ESC unit. Problems here will cause trouble too. Look out for low voltage at pin eight as well as at the coil.

Earth and voltage checks should be carried out under load, and Frank interprets this to mean testing with the engine running or during cranking. The latter is preferable as far as he is concerned because the loading is greater. In a good circuit there should be no more than a one volt drop.

One final problem associated with this application, but not one relating specifically to the ignition system, causes engine stalling and a lean mixture with misfires. The problem can be with either the fuel cut-off solenoid or the idle jet within the carburettor.

Frank says that the condition of the idle jet does have a significant influence on the air/fuel mixture through the primary choke range. The extra fuel this jet supplies does make a difference so its efficient operation is important. The solenoid valve plays a vital role too and any problems with this should be dealt with by replacement.

NEXT MONTH
Vauxhall Omega V6.

ELECTRONIC DIAGNOSTICS!

Tracing and fixing faults in electronic engine management systems

Number 55: *Vauxhall's Carlton/Senator replacement, the Omega, is around in large numbers now and the V6 version can represent great value for money. But what of its electrical manners? Chris Graham finds out.*

Bosch Motronic is a well-proven and successful management system which has been chosen by a number of quality car manufacturers for many years now. It's developed with the times, become steadily more complex and now really is an 'all-singing, all-dancing' engine manager.

TYPICAL FAULTS
1. **HT leads**
2. **Lambda sensors**
3. **EGR valve**

The M2.8.1 version is utilised by Vauxhall's X25XE and X30XE engines in the Omega V6 2.5 and 3.0-litre models. It's a variation on the Motronic theme, falling in between M2.8, used on the Cavalier V6, and M2.8.3, found on the latest big-engined Vectras.

Frank Massey, independent tuning expert and proprietor of Fuel Injection Services (Tel: 01772 201597), is an admirer of Motronic but is the first to admit that M2.8.1 is a complex system. He says it's not particularly technician-

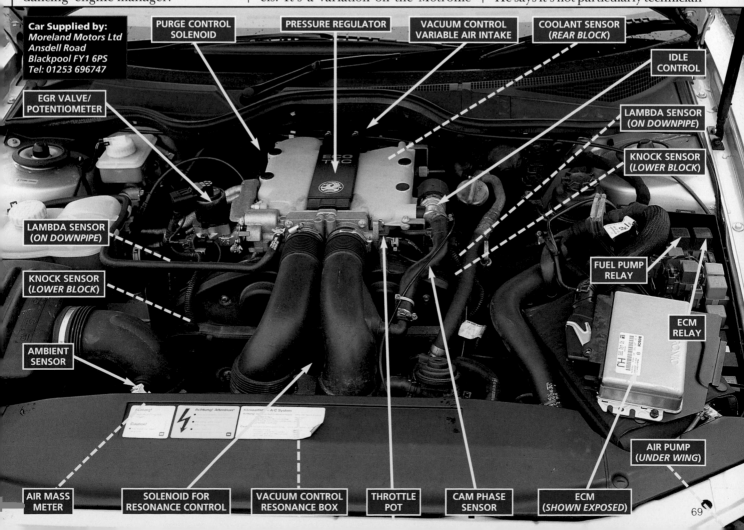

Car Supplied by:
*Moreland Motors Ltd
Ansdell Road
Blackpool FY1 6PS
Tel: 01253 696747*

PURGE CONTROL SOLENOID

PRESSURE REGULATOR

VACUUM CONTROL VARIABLE AIR INTAKE

COOLANT SENSOR (*REAR BLOCK*)

IDLE CONTROL

EGR VALVE/ POTENTIOMETER

LAMBDA SENSOR (*ON DOWNPIPE*)

KNOCK SENSOR (*LOWER BLOCK*)

LAMBDA SENSOR (*ON DOWNPIPE*)

KNOCK SENSOR (*LOWER BLOCK*)

FUEL PUMP RELAY

ECM RELAY

AMBIENT SENSOR

AIR MASS METER

SOLENOID FOR RESONANCE CONTROL

VACUUM CONTROL RESONANCE BOX

THROTTLE POT

CAM PHASE SENSOR

ECM (*SHOWN EXPOSED*)

AIR PUMP (*UNDER WING*)

IGNITION MANAGEMENT

This system has just about everything you can imagine. It's a full engine management package which controls ignition and fuelling from a single 55-pin ECU located in the engine bay, close to the battery. There is a triple coil pack (providing 'wasted spark' ignition) driven directly by the ECU.

Major components include: a crank angle sensor; a camshaft phase sensor; a conventional coolant sensor; an ambient air temperature sensor; a throttle potentiometer; an air mass meter (on the induction side); a rotary idle control valve; twin Lambda sensors (one in each downpipe); six sequentially-controlled solenoid injectors; twin knock sensors.

Added to these basic components are: a secondary air induction system, with an air pump found under the front n/s wing, to aid cold start performance and emissions, controlled directly by the ECU; a carbon canister solenoid valve; an ECU-controlled variable induction manifold; an exhaust gas recirculation (EGR) system.

There are other potential inputs from areas such as the automatic transmission (almost always fitted), ABS and/or traction control, air conditioning and power steering. It's all very complex!

Having said all this, Frank adds that most of the problems so far encountered relate to simple and predictable causes, so all is not lost.

There is the potential for serial communications on this application, using a suitable piece of test equipment, such as Sykes-Pickavant's excellent Advanced Code Reader. Access is simple (via a J1962 socket under the steering column) and opens the door to a great deal of useful information. Many of the components can be 'driven' by a code reader – including the tank vent valve, intake manifold solenoid, the air pump and the EGR valve – to test their functionality.

It's also possible to gather a reasonable amount of data – voltage values – as seen by the ECU, which can be particularly useful for tracking down broken wires etc.

If any codes present themselves, Frank suggests that you make a note of each, clear them, and drive the car to see if any return. Don't automatically assume that everything you find at the first attempt represents a genuine fault.

There is always the possibility that some may have been installed by default – often by somebody removing a wire and re-connecting it, for example, or resulting from electrical interference. Any which return after clearing must be taken seriously and dealt with as genuine faults.

Without a code reader your only realistic method of gathering data is by using a breakout box and oscilloscope on the ECU. This is made easy because the ECU can be removed simply on its slide plate, and there are bags of spare wiring.

If you have no diagnostic equipment at all you can 'bridge out' pins 5 and 6 in the OBD2 socket under the steering column, using a piece of wire. This will engage the blink code system and flash any stored codes via a dash light. This is of limited value because it simply displays all faults as total failures, which, of course, they may not be.

Frank says that this system can suffer greatly from components which are running out of specification, but still within the parameters of fault code triggering. The only way to assess such a situation is by gaining access to 'live' data, using an oscilloscope.

friendly, with accessibility to the most common service parts (plugs, coil pack, belts etc) being extremely restricted.

It is a technically sophisticated system which interfaces with ABS braking, transmission and alarm systems. From an electrical reliability point of view Frank says the car is not old enough yet to draw any definitive conclusions. But from what he has seen so far, in particular the wiring layout and location of the earth points, the likelihood is that problems will arise as the years pass. The demands on a modern system like this are such that it takes very little to tip the balance and cause trouble.

PREPARATION

This is involved for these engines. Most will have racked up a reasonably high mileage before they even enter the independent specialist sector, so your first port of call should always be the HT leads. The condition of these is critical because there are so many other electrical systems present that the potential for electrical interference is great. Be guided by the condition of the plugs and leads. They can tell you a great deal about how an engine is performing.

Remove the plugs which, in itself, is no easy task. Frank says that the leads are extremely difficult to get to, being tightly clipped into place and covered by various runs of conduit. If you find a plug showing the tell-tale sign of a brown stained corona ring around the base of its porcelain body, then this

means that electrical tracking has been taking place. The leads will certainly need to be changed. The lead itself should confirm the problem. If you inspect up inside the plug end, you will usually see white or yellow powdery deposits, which signify that electrical 'flash over' has been taking place.

The problem is that to replace the plug leads you have to carry out a lot of dismantling work. First, the plastic mouldings which run across the back of the engine bay, immediately under the screen, must be removed. The plenum chamber must come off the top of the engine, together with several air induction hoses, vacuum hoses and other breather devices. Only then can you reach down the back of the block to gain access to the coil. Even then, physically changing the leads remains difficult.

All this work must be undertaken

carefully. The last thing you want is to put it all back together and find that you have created an air leak somewhere in the system. These can be very difficult to track down. Also remember that while everything is stripped down, a number of extremely important apertures will be exposed – especially on the air inlet side. Block all of these with clean rags or paper towels to prevent foreign bodies sneaking in where they shouldn't.

Elsewhere, take a close look at all vacuum hoses and use a mirror and torch where necessary. Most of this inspection is best done during the plug changing operations, when many of the obstructions have been removed.

Wash the idle control valve out carefully using carburettor cleaner. The inlet track tends to remain fairly clean on these engines, but Frank advises

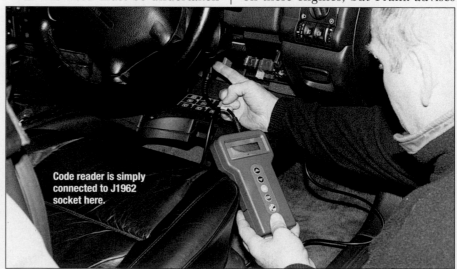

Code reader is simply connected to J1962 socket here.

ELECTRONIC DIAGNOSTICS!

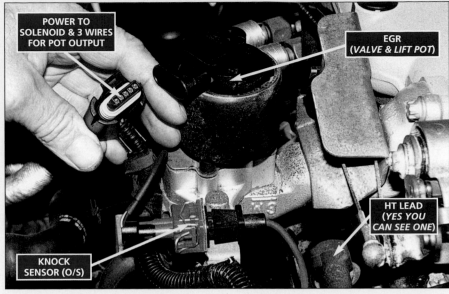

POWER TO SOLENOID & 3 WIRES FOR POT OUTPUT

EGR (VALVE & LIFT POT)

HT LEAD (YES YOU CAN SEE ONE)

KNOCK SENSOR (O/S)

checking it nonetheless. Check also the main air induction pick-ups at the front. These are essentially large-bore hoses, but you should make sure they are not damaged and that their O rings are tight and correctly located.

VAUXHALL VICES

The most common fault which Frank has come across on the V6-powered Omega models so far relates to HT leads. It presents itself as engine hesitation and misfire. The latter can be very subtle on a multi-cylinder engine like this, and therefore difficult to detect.

If there is electrical 'flash-over' across the leads to the head or down the lead to the base of the plug, no matter how experienced you are, they can be incredibly difficult to detect, even using an oscilloscope. Really, the only advice that Frank can offer here is to change the leads. Don't mess about spending ages trying to track down the problem, replace the leads with quality, original equipment products, and swap the plugs too.

If this type of problem goes unchecked then there can be serious knock-on effects to worry about. A by-product of misfires is unburnt fuel and this is a deadly enemy of the catalytic converter. Frank believes there are two on this application so replacement could be a costly business. Under normal circumstances, catalysts will usually last for about 80,000 miles. But with the addition of unburnt fuel, this life will be significantly shortened.

Another misfire-related problem can be caused by trouble with the coil pack. This, as I've already mentioned, is tucked well away at the back of the engine, close to the bulkhead. Unfortunately, its positioning, apart from making it extremely awkward to get at, also exposes it to attack from water running down off the screen.

The plastic panelling which runs across the width of the car, under the screen, appears to lose its ability to divert all the run off away to the sides. Part of the problem could well be that these panels are the ones which have to be removed when changing the HT leads and, once they have been in and out

a few times, their fit can suffer. Frank says that they simply butt together, so it doesn't take much stress-induced distortion to open up a gap. Also, it may be that if the engine bay has been steam cleaned or jet washed 'over enthusiastically' – water might have been forced down into this critical area.

Recently Frank came across a typical example where the coil pack was producing a perfectly good spark, but the voltage was tracking down the outside of the coil pack body and seeping away to earth, rather than going to the plug. This created a violent misfire on one cylinder only.

Having removed the coil, one terminal was found to be extremely rusty. The insulation had broken down completely due to spark erosion and normal operation was impossible. Water ingress was the probable cause, although Frank wondered if poor fitting of the plug lead on to the coil terminal could have been an additional factor. If the rubber boot had not been secured effectively over the tower then water ingress would be assured.

The only solution was to replace the coil pack and fit a new set of leads. Frank undertook this particular job for a local Vauxhall dealer and so cannot be sure of parts prices. But he estimates that the coil pack costs about £100, plus £160 or so for a set of leads.

There is not much you can do to avoid this problem, apart from keeping an eye on the condition of the coil pack. Do your best to keep the body of the pack clean and dry. Oily deposits should be removed using a clean cloth and suitable solvent. If you are at all suspicious about the condition of the rubber boots on the leads then replace them, making sure the new ones are pushed fully home.

The second problem highlighted by Frank concerns vehicles which may be found to lack power and smoothness, coupled with poor fuel consumption. His first move, with these symptoms, is to test the operation of the two Lambda sensors. It is important to check both and not to assume that the pair are fine simply because the first you try is switching correctly.

The easiest way to gain access to these is from underneath. Lift the vehicle and clip on to the wires from below so that the voltage output can be measured. The switching is standard over a range of 0.2-0.8V, at a minimum frequency of 1Hz (once a second). Ideally, a good sensor should be

TECHNICAL SPECIFICATIONS

Component	Output	ECU pin
Crank angle sensor	A/C signal, 10V min, peak-to-peak, at idle	49
	Ground	48
Coolant temp. sensor	3.5V cold, 1V hot	45
Air temp. sensor	3.5V cold, 2-3V hot	44
Throttle position sensor	0.5V closed, 4.5V open throt.	53
Lambda sensor (1)	0.2-0.8V @ 1Hz minimum	28
Lambda sensor (2)	0.2-0.8V @ 1Hz minimum	47
Secondary air pump	12V off, Ground on	26
Air mass meter	1V idle, 4V+ snap load	7
Camshaft ID sensor	A/C signal, 10V min, peak-to-peak, at idle	8
EGR lift pot.	0.5V closed, 3.5V+ open	50
Charcoal solenoid	12V off, Ground on	5
Idle control valve	Digital 12V/0V signal 100Hz duty controlled	4
Fuel injectors (approx.)	Saturated pulse, one per cycle. Cold crank 12-16ms, cold 4-5ms, hot 3-4ms, snap load 12ms	
	Injector 1	17
	Injector 2	16
	Injector 3	35
	Injector 4	34
	Injector 5	15
	Injector 6	33

BOSCH MOTRONIC M2.8.1

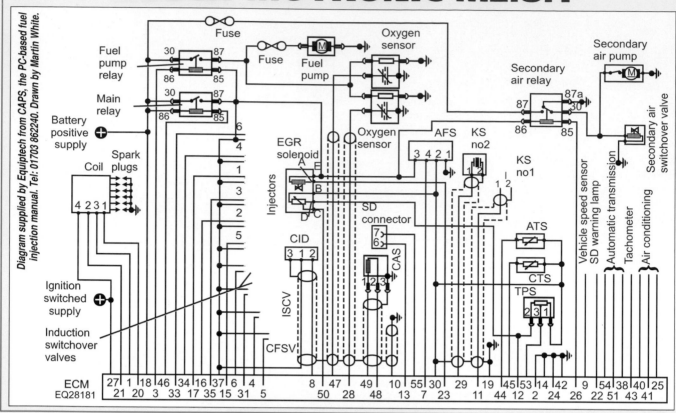

Diagram supplied by Equiptech from CAPS, the PC-based fuel injection manual. Tel: 01703 862240. Drawn by Martin White.

switching more quickly, at 2-3Hz.

If the switching is found to be poor, and you opt to fit replacements, then consider wiring up additional earth connections as well (direct to battery negative). Often this will prove very beneficial, particularly if the car is an older example. It's also sensible to check that the Lambda sensor signals are actually being 'seen' by the ECU. The simplest way to do this is to use a code reader to capture serial data on sensor output.

Sometimes you can change the sensors and still find them not switching as they should. If this is the case, and performance continues to be 'flat', especially when being driven hard, then Frank's suggestion is that the catalytic converters may well be partially or totally blocked.

The most efficent way to diagnose this is by using a vacuum gauge attached to the inlet manifold (there are a number of convenient points to 'T' into). Drive the car down the road at high load with a steady throttle and check for a healthy manifold vacuum (20-22inHg). If it is not, and it decays as load increases, then this will point strongly towards a problem with the cats.

Remember that if you have to replace the cats, then make sure the cause of the problem (be it unburnt fuel resulting from a misfire) is cured, otherwise the same thing will happen again.

The final fault we'll look at here concerns the EGR valve. This is a mechan-

ical device which lifts and allows exhaust gases to be ducted back into the air intake. It is a duty cycle control valve, which means that it operates in accordance with the demands of engine load.

Whether this valve operates efficiently or not depends upon whether it remains able to move freely. Unfortunately, it has a tendency to become con-

taminated with carbon deposits which eventually make its action sticky and sluggish. This impairs its movement and so even though correct signals are arriving from the ECU, problems arise.

The effects will be felt even before the valve actually grinds to a halt. Erratic movement will cause the valve's potentiometer to send spurious and confusing voltage outputs to the ECU.

The on-the-road effects of this will be a reduction in power, especially under load, and a very uneven idle. Under normal circumstances the EGR valve should not operate during idle, so if it becomes stuck open, idle quality falls away dramatically.

Valve operation should be checked by connecting a voltmeter or oscilloscope to the EGR's potentiometer. When monitoring output in this way you should see a smooth transition across the voltage range (0.5-4V). Remember also, that during normal working, this valve gets hot because it is located on the exhaust flange, so test it hot, not cold.

The bad news is that EGR valves can rarely be cleaned effectively once they have become contaminated. Frank says it may be worth having a go with ultrasonics but the likelihood is that a replacement will be required. The cost of this is about £170.

NEXT MONTH
Rover 214

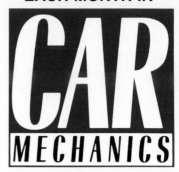
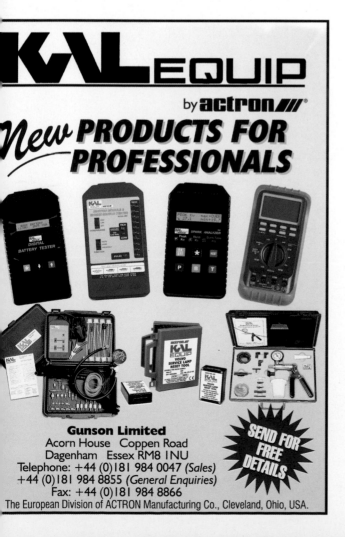
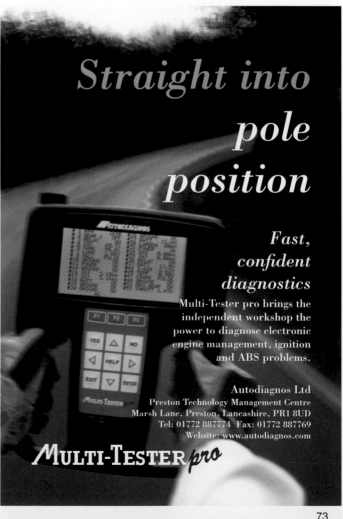

ELECTRONIC DIAGNOSTICS!

Tracing and fixing faults in electronic engine management systems

Number 56: *The Peugeot 306 is such a popular car here now that it's high time we considered its electrical behaviour. Chris Graham reports.*

Like so many other high-volume hatchbacks, the Peugeot 306 has seen many engine management changes over its successful production life to date. In fact, one of the biggest problems when dealing with a troublesome 306 is actually identifying which system is fitted!

The range is split between Bosch and Magneti-Marelli systems, with dif-

POTENTIAL PROBLEMS
1. **Faulty sockets**
2. **MAP sensor pipe**
3. **HT leads**

ferent versions of each appearing, depending on engine size and age. The car featured here is a popular 1.6-litre model running Bosch Motronic MP5.1, which first appeared in 1992.

This system is also found on 1.8-litre versions, and on the larger but older 405 1.8. Later variants of the 306 will be found with MP5.2 but the differences are only slight. The way to determine management system type is by using a dedicated code reader to interrogate the ECU's identification coding. This really is the only way to be sure about what you are dealing with.

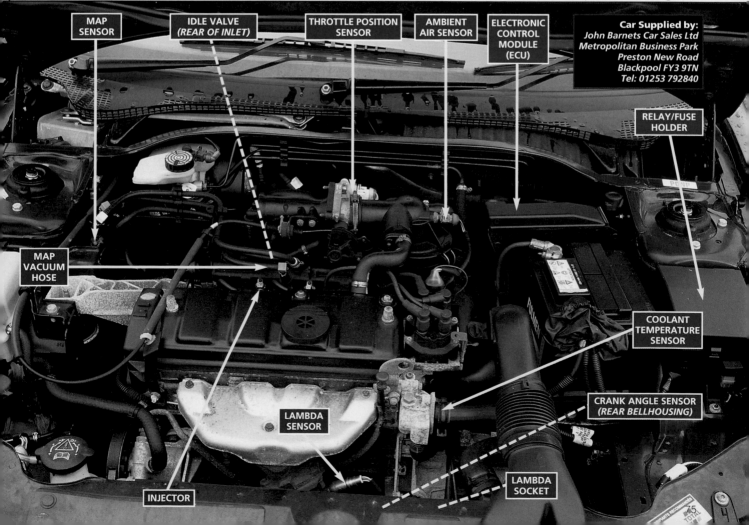

MAP SENSOR

IDLE VALVE (REAR OF INLET)

THROTTLE POSITION SENSOR

AMBIENT AIR SENSOR

ELECTRONIC CONTROL MODULE (ECU)

Car Supplied by:
*John Barnets Car Sales Ltd
Metropolitan Business Park
Preston New Road
Blackpool FY3 9TN
Tel: 01253 792840*

RELAY/FUSE HOLDER

MAP VACUUM HOSE

COOLANT TEMPERATURE SENSOR

LAMBDA SENSOR

CRANK ANGLE SENSOR (REAR BELLHOUSING)

INJECTOR

LAMBDA SOCKET

ENGINE MANAGEMENT

This system provides total engine management with multi-point fuel injection coupled to a DIS ignition system with double-ended coils. The coil pack is mounted at one end of the cylinder head.

The ECU has a curious specification. The unit has a 55-pin socket, similar to other Bosch set-ups, with the pins arranged in three rows. However, only two rows are actually used.

There is a typical arrangement of components which include: an air temperature sensor in the air induction system; an NTC coolant temperature sensor in the water jacket at the back of the head; a remote MAP sensor on the o/s inner wing which looks very like a small ignition module; a road speed sensor; a Lambda sensor mounted as usual in the downpipe at the front of the engine; a crank angle sensor picking up off the flywheel; an idle control valve at the rear of the engine, under the inlet manifold; four conventional fuel injectors; either a composite or separate relays; a throttle position indicator on the throttle housing; a manifold pre-heater; a charcoal canister solenoid for purging the fuel tank of evaporated gases and a fuel pump located within the tank.

The car is fitted with an encryption alarm system which immobilises the engine. There is a transponder in the ignition key which relays a code to the receiver located around the ignition lock barrel. This sends a signal to a separate alarm ECU, which, in turn, forwards this to the main engine ECU, assuming all is well. There has to be agreement all the way along the chain before the engine will be allowed to start.

There is code reading potential on this system, with access being gained via a 16-pin OBD2 socket. This, in common with an increasing number of modern cars, is found on this Peugeot under the steering column, just above the driver's left knee position.

From this socket it is possible to read stored fault codes, clear them, drive selected actuators (injectors, idle control valve, assorted solenoids etc) and to observe live data. It will check on output values from temperature sensors, fuel injectors (durations) and timing position.

There is a warning light on the dashboard to indicate when engine management-related faults have been detected.

Frank Massey, our expert guide to all things electronic and proprietor of Preston-based Fuel Injection Services (Tel: 01772 201597), is generally impressed with this system, although he admits it does have its share of niggly problems. The overall layout under the bonnet is reasonably good. The engine is small within the bay so there is plenty of room to work.

The ECU is located in a box on the nearside of the engine and there are no long wiring runs to worry about, or potentially troublesome apertures through bulkheads etc. It's a multipoint system, which, in Frank's opinion, is certainly preferable to the 'asthmatic' singlepoint alternative and generally he reports that reliability levels are good.

PREPARATION

The idle control valve should be one of your prime areas of attention as far as general preparation is concerned. Frank's advice is that this should always be removed, as a matter of course, so that it can be carefully washed out

and dried, together with the main air intake to the throttle housing.

Also pay particular attention to the condition of the coil pack. The forward location of this makes it rather vulnerable to dirt and water contamination and even on the car we looked at, which was essentially very clean, the top of this crucial component was suffering in this way. The system operates on a fairly high output and electrical tracking will definitely take place given the slightest provocation.

Check the condition and cleanliness of the HT leads too. The section which fits down over the plug is the really crucial part. While not being an especially long lead, they can nevertheless suffer from debris down in the plug aperture which might become conductive. You may also find a build-up of white powder within the plug end of the lead. This can be conductive as well, leading to misfires caused by electrical shunts down the lead and across the plug.

If you are in any doubt about the condition of the leads then always opt to fit a new set. It's important to specify quality replacements – Frank's advice is always to use original equipment specification, then there can be no doubt about lead performance.

In most cases the leads will be OK and will only require a thorough wash and dry before being re-fitted. Make sure that the plug apertures are clean and that the right sort of plug is fitted. It should be a resistive type with the correct heat range and suitable gap.

It may also be well worth removing the vacuum sampling pipe, at the MAP sensor end, to check that it is clear right back to the engine. There is a T-piece junction closer to the engine so check this carefully. Remember always to blow back in the direction of the engine. Never do so towards the MAP sensor itself or you will seriously damage it.

Essentially this engine is normally a

These two plug connectors, one for the Lambda sensor and the other for the crank angle sensor, suffer badly from dirt and water contamination.

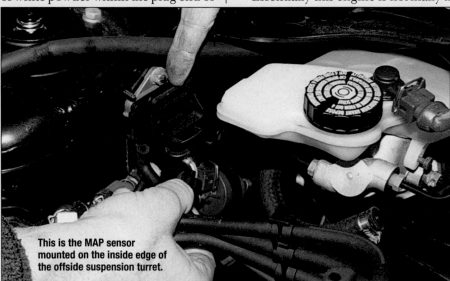

This is the MAP sensor mounted on the inside edge of the offside suspension turret.

ELECTRONIC DIAGNOSTICS!

very clean unit, with little oil contamination and no water problems to worry about. Consequently, preparation is a relatively simple business.

PEUGEOT POSERS!

The first problem to consider relates to faulty sockets. There are two in particular on this car, which, because of their location, suffer badly from dirt and water ingress. They are found right down on the front nearside of the engine and both are absolutely crucial to the operation of the whole system.

The one on the left (as you face the engine from the front) is for the Lambda sensor and is a four-wire socket. The crank angle sensor has a three-pin socket – output, ground and screen.

Failure of the crank angle sensor means failure of the engine, it's as simple as that. Intermittent problems with this component will be sufficient to cause severe juddering or even momentary cutting out. Failure of the Lambda sensor will cause problems with the fuelling, but the nature of these will depend on the way in which it fails.

If the signal is lost completely the ECU will 'see' this as a 'go rich' signal and the engine will run badly and smoke noticeably. There is also a likelihood, under rich mixture conditions, that the sensor will become sooted-up which will stop it switching and possibly lead to catalyst damage.

Alternatively, if it defaults 'high' then the resultant 'go lean' signal will cause the mixture to be weakened too much, producing a flat engine with poor response and acceleration.

So if you discover problems with crank angle sensor output, outright failure, or intermittent signals, then the first job should be to strip the socket. The same applies to a badly switching Lambda. Take the sockets apart in both cases and make sure that the pins are thoroughly clean. A sensible precaution in Frank's experience is to dab on a thin coating of Vaseline, to help prevent similar problems in the future.

Both these troubles can be logged by the ECU as a stored fault code, and the dash light will be triggered. However, often the intermittent nature of the

Code reader socket found under steering column – standardised position on modern vehicles.

problem means that the ECU will not recognise the fault soon enough and so none will actually be recorded, even though driveability is usually adversely affected.

Frank says that quite often these faults will only be coded under 'closed loop' conditions. So if the car is used predominantly in a way which leads to 'open loop' operation – during warm up, town driving, vigorous acceleration and slowing down etc – it probably won't be recorded at all. Prolonged cruising, however, should highlight the trouble.

The solution is to check the sensor outputs by voltage. This can be done simply with a code reader, and the advantage of this approach is that you will be monitoring exactly what the ECU is 'seeing'. In this way you will be taking into account the component, the wiring and the way in which the ECU is interpreting the information.

We mentioned in the preparation notes that the rubber pipe running between the engine and the MAP sensor should be checked on a regular basis for blockages and contamination.

Well, in some cases you may well find a more serious problem relating to this important length of vacuum hose.

This pipe runs through a tight, pre-shaped bend at the MAP sensor end, very close to the component. Frank has come across instances where it's been damaged at this point, badly enough to prevent the vacuum being passed. He's not sure of the exact cause – possibly engine movement – but the knock-on effect will be a rich engine which, in the worst cases, will hardly run.

Most recently he was actually straining the pipe and using a small mirror to inspect its condition when he discovered a tiny split on the bend. Despite being small, it was quite sufficient to cause a drop in pressure and thus, the rich mixture. Other possible causes include careless handling when the pipe is being removed or unintentional levering from a tool. Obviously the MAP sensor output is critical, and this can also be easily read using a code reader.

In many cases Frank says that the system will recover once the pipe has been replaced. The Lambda will usually start to switch again and, with luck, the catalyst will not have been damaged too severely either. This backs up the case for not assuming that simply because a Lambda sensor is not switching as it should, it must be unserviceable.

Serious problems with HT leads are becoming much more common now according to Frank. They become conductive, for whatever reason, and lose spark voltage down the outside of the plug to create poor, hesitant performance. The biggest give-away of this condition is the presence of a brownish 'corona' ring around the base of the plug. This staining indicates that electrical 'flashover' is taking place and should

TECHNICAL SPECIFICATIONS

Component/function	Technical data
Coolant temp sensor	Cold 3.8V, hot 1.0V
Ambient air temp sensor	Cold 3.5V, hot 2.5V
Throttle pot (3-wire)	Closed 0.5V, fully open 4.5V 5V supply
MAP sensor	Static 4.5V, 5in/Hg 3.8V, 10in/Hg 2.9V, 15in/Hg 2.0V 20in/Hg 1.2V
Lambda sensor	0.2-0.8V @ 1Hz
Crank angle sensor	AC signal, minimum 10V peak to peak at idle, 5V minimum when cranking
Idle control valve	Digital switch, 12V/0V @ 100Hz Duty controlled Duty 25% hot idle, 45% cold idle, 75% cranking
Fuel injector duration	Cold 3.5ms, hot 2.2ms, Snap load 8-12+ms

Plug leads can deteriorate with age. Check ends
of extensions for white powdery deposits.

always be viewed with suspicion.

Even if the plugs are not very old
they will have to be changed because
without some new components the
problem is not going to go away. Frank
would also suggest that the leads be replaced too. He adds that simply changing the plugs may eradicate the problem for a few thousand miles, but this
is simply because the new plug will
have lowered the firing voltage. Trouble will return as soon as the plug voltage begins to rise. Usually the problem
lies with the lead.

Frank says that he has also come
across a few 306s with faulty throttle
potentiometers, which can create similar driveability problems and bad
idling characteristics. Much depends
on how the pot. actually fails. In theory
a code reader should identify this type
of problem, but often the fault comes
and goes too quickly for the ECU to
catch and register it as a code.

The only solution is to check the out-

put carefully, right across the range,
using a suitable oscilloscope. Don't neglect the wiring either – it could be this
causing the problem, rather than a fault
with the pot. itself. Give it all a good
wiggle around and bear in mind that
engine movement could be sufficient
to aggravate a faulty wire sufficiently.
It could also be a heat-related problem
so check the outputs under varying
conditions to cover all the possibilities.

If you conclude that the pot. itself is

at fault then replacement is the only solution. A modification to throttle pot.
specification was made earlier in this
system's life, so check with your dealer
to make sure which is fitted. Most
newer cars should be equipped with
the latest unit. If needed, a replacement will cost about £50.

TYPICAL PEUGEOT MOTRONIC 5.1

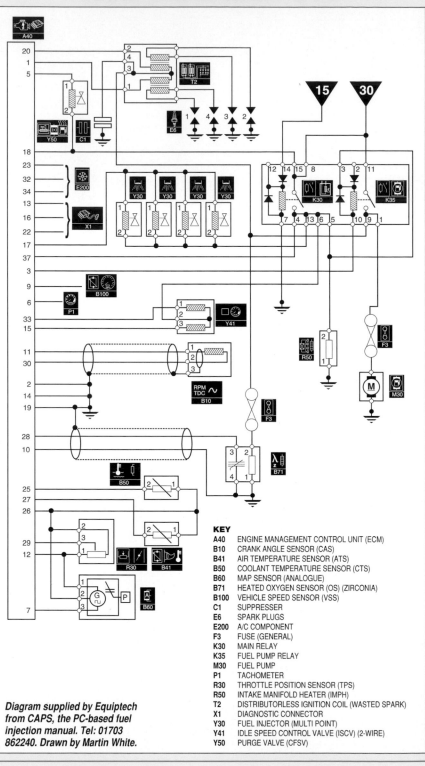

Diagram supplied by Equiptech
from CAPS, the PC-based fuel
injection manual. Tel: 01703
862240. Drawn by Martin White.

KEY

A40	ENGINE MANAGEMENT CONTROL UNIT (ECM)
B10	CRANK ANGLE SENSOR (CAS)
B41	AIR TEMPERATURE SENSOR (ATS)
B50	COOLANT TEMPERATURE SENSOR (CTS)
B60	MAP SENSOR (ANALOGUE)
B71	HEATED OXYGEN SENSOR (OS) (ZIRCONIA)
B100	VEHICLE SPEED SENSOR (VSS)
C1	SUPPRESSER
E6	SPARK PLUGS
E200	A/C COMPONENT
F3	FUSE (GENERAL)
K30	MAIN RELAY
K35	FUEL PUMP RELAY
M30	FUEL PUMP
P1	TACHOMETER
R30	THROTTLE POSITION SENSOR (TPS)
R50	INTAKE MANIFOLD HEATER (IMPH)
T2	DISTRIBUTORLESS IGNITION COIL (WASTED SPARK)
X1	DIAGNOSTIC CONNECTOR
Y30	FUEL INJECTOR (MULTI POINT)
Y41	IDLE SPEED CONTROL VALVE (ISCV) (2-WIRE)
Y50	PURGE VALVE (CFSV)

NEXT MONTH

ROVER 214.

78

ELECTRONIC DIAGNOSTICS!

Tracing and fixing faults in electronic engine management systems

Number 57: *The Rover 214 represents very affordable motoring, but are things so encouraging from a diagnostics point of view? Chris Graham finds out.*

The Rover MEMS (Modular Engine Management System) is a multi-point set-up which has been around for ages and, consequently, is to be found governing a whole host of different Rover applications, including the latest Mini Cooper, 100, 200 and 400 Series cars. The system itself has not altered significantly over its service life, although it is continually being enhanced with electrical

POTENTIAL PROBLEMS
1. **ECU faults**
2. **Lambda sensor**
3. **MAP sensor**

tweaks here and there!

Frank Massey, who runs Preston-based Fuel Injection Services (Tel: 01772 201597) and advises us on all things electronic, considers it to be a competent system overall. However,

he admits that an increasing number of problems are starting to appear now, and that these have multiplied noticeably in the past couple of years.

The system has its characteristic weaknesses but, fortunately, Frank reports that there is nothing to be unduly concerned about. Accessibility under the bonnet is excellent. This may seem a basic point but it's a luxury which is becoming increasingly rare on modern

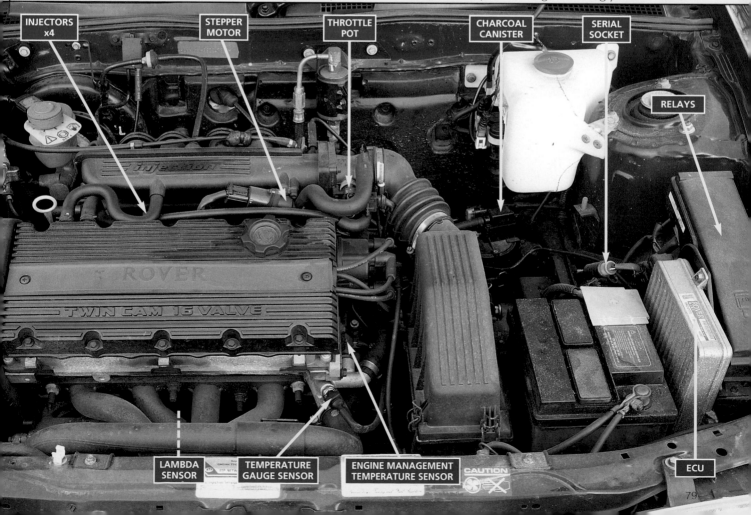

INJECTORS x4 · STEPPER MOTOR · THROTTLE POT · CHARCOAL CANISTER · SERIAL SOCKET · RELAYS · ROVER · Injection · TWIN CAM 16 VALVE · LAMBDA SENSOR · TEMPERATURE GAUGE SENSOR · ENGINE MANAGEMENT TEMPERATURE SENSOR · CAUTION · ECU

ENGINE MANAGEMENT

Rover MEMS is a total engine management system with fuel and ignition control provided by a single ECU. The control unit, which is found under the bonnet on all applications, drives the coil directly (no module fitted). The primary input to the ECU comes from the crank angle sensor, which determines engine position thus allowing calculations about injector and coil firing to be made. The coolant sensor provides the main temperature input to the ECU, but is supported by fuel temperature and ambient air sensors. All three are 'negative coefficient' sensors producing a variable voltage output.

Other significant components include: a knock sensor in the block; an inertia switch, which breaks the power supply to the fuel pump; a plunger-type stepper motor for idle speed control which is driven directly by the ECU; a throttle poten-

tiometer and four Bosch fuel injectors which are supplied via an in-tank pump, through a fuel rail with pressure regulator. Relay arrangement may vary depending on application. The options are either a set of three individual relays or a multi-function unit (MFU), which combines a number of relays in one sealed component. The smaller vehicle applications tend to make use of the MFU, while the 200 and 400 models are usually fitted with separate relays, as in this case. Frank prefers the latter, simply because problems with the MFU mean the whole thing has to be replaced, rather than just a single, cheaper relay. Some later vehicles will be fitted with an encrypted alarm system.

To make any significant tuning adjustments to fuelling or ignition, there are two separate approaches. The fuel side of the system must be tackled, assuming that the

car is not fitted with a catalytic converter, by using a serial communicator. This will allow you to set the mixture and base idle. To look at ignition you will need a more standard engine tuner.

A serial communicator will also allow you access to any fault codes which may be present, and enable you to drive various actuators (injectors, stepper motor etc). The codes cannot be accessed in any other way – there is no blink light on the dash. The other big advantage of using a code reader is that it will allow you to assess the performance of the MAP sensor, which is mounted internally within the ECU. The inputs the ECU is 'seeing' will be displayed as pressure values, and these can be compared with actual values taken from the engine using a vacuum gauge. Obviously, the two should be the same.

cars these days.

There's good news on the wiring front too. Frank cannot recall a single significant fault in this respect, and in his opinion the quality of the components used is generally good. As a final general point, Frank says that he has noticed an increasing trend for MEMS ECUs to develop characteristically common faults. These centre around fuel injector and stepper motor outputs, but can also relate to the MAP sensor, which is internal within the control unit. Replacement ECUs for this application cost about £120.

PREPARATION

The relative simplicity of the MEMS system ensures that the preparation needed is never usually that involved. The engines remain essentially clean, which helps, but Frank says that the older models are getting to an age now when physical abuse is starting to take its toll.

A particularly common occurrence is damage to the plug leads. They are fitted quite deep down into the head, and feature a plastic support sleeve which can suffer from cracking if handled carelessly. The original equipment Rover leads are of a perfectly good quality and Frank has no hesitation in recommending them when replacements are needed.

However, as an alternative, he has found out that Ford XR3i leads fit extremely well too and are, if anything, of slightly better quality. Often he will fit these, adding that they are much cheaper as well! Always wash out the plug apertures and then check the distributor cap and rotor, making sure that the arm fitted is of the later variety. If you find one with a steel bush or

NEED TRAINING?
Frank Massey runs regular courses at his well-equipped Preston workshop; everything from basic engine management introductions to full-blown, 'hands on', system-specific tuition.
Call 01772 201597 for details.

insert, it's an early one and should be ditched. They are prone to tracking, leading to a poor spark. The later version has a body made entirely from plastic and is much more durable accordingly. If in any doubt then fit a new distributor cap as well.

Frank says that he is starting to see a few oil-contaminated caps, usually caused by the rear camshaft oil seal starting to leak. In such cases you have to consider whether simply changing the cap is the real answer, without dealing with the worn oil seal, which will only get worse if ignored.

The coil is located rather vulnerably down at the front of the engine on the inner wing. It can suffer with dirt and water contamination. In some cases you may find a rubber boot fitted over the coil, but Frank does not believe these help at all. He always cuts them off, arguing that it's far better for the coil to be exposed and washed regu-

larly than covered and ignored.

There is a vacuum pipe which runs to the ECU and this is nearly always contaminated with fuel or oil. It should be blown through carefully with an air line, but always back in the direction of the engine. There is also a petrol trap fitted to most applications which should be emptied or renewed at this stage. Try not to blow through this with the air line because the pressure is likely to destroy it.

If you find that the pipe has deteriorated in any way – become soft, chafed or split – then change it. Also pay attention to its fitting at the ECU end. This is a potentially weak point. The plastic extension on to which the pipe locates is easily snapped off by careless handling, so be warned. If you find that the pipe is a loose fit then cut it back to an unstretched section and re-fit.

Normally, the throttle body will be relatively clean but it's good practice to wash it out with carburettor cleaner all the same. The throttle stop is rarely touched and the potentiometer is not adjustable, so no attention should be required by these.

The stepper motor is essentially reliable too. It can only be adjusted via

Rotor arm was updated to an all-plastic design a while ago. Always opt for this latest spec when replacing.

ELECTRONIC DIAGNOSTICS!

serial communications, but its action is governed by a stop on the throttle linkage. This should only be tackled as part of a serial communications 'tune-up' procedure.

WHAT GOES WRONG?

The ECU is becoming a relatively common cause of trouble on these MEMS-equipped Rovers. The problem is that in most cases these faults, being internal, are uncorrectable and so the only solution is a replacement control unit. However, a further complication is that they can be difficult to diagnose.

Frank says a frequent defect he comes across relates to the stepper motor drive signal. This can be a particularly difficult one to track down because of the unusual nature of the signal. It's not like a conventional, clear-cut digital output with defined amplitude and frequency. The stepper is operated by what's called a 'pulse width modulated control', which means that it receives inputs of varying duration and frequency. Therefore, there is no such thing as a good or bad signal.

The value of the signal is determined by how much the throttle needs to be opened, which is part of the computer programme built into the ECU. It's impossible to quote figures for it and when you look at the waveform displayed on an oscilloscope, it can appear very complicated. Frank admits that even he sometimes has problems determining whether or not the signal he's observing is at the root of a problem.

The 'on the road' symptoms of such a defect are engine stalling, poor fast idle and bad idle response. As a guideline, from a diagnostics point of view, if the supply to the stepper motor is good (12V) then your next move should be to check the earth values. The quality of the control lies in the reference to earth, and this takes place internally through the ECU. If these are suspect then the fault lies with the ECU itself. Ensure good ECM ground at pin 29. This is usually the case and Frank cannot actually recall a single instance when he has needed to change a stepper. The motor itself is a very simple device and it can be driven for testing purposes, using a code reader.

An additional problem is that,

in Frank's experience, testing ECUs is not as clear-cut as it might be. He and colleagues have had problems when faulty ECUs have passed simulated tests successfully, only for the problem on the car to remain. The only sure-fire solution is to swap it for a professionally reconditioned replacement.

Frank says that quite a number of these MEMS-equipped Rovers are starting to fail the MoT test on emissions. Usually the problem is that they are running too rich and this will often be traced to a poor Lambda sensor switch. This sensor can fail in a variety of ways, to ground or at an output of 0.8V, for example. Defects of this sort will throw the system into 'limp home' mode.

However, the cause is not always a faulty sensor and so you need to check its operation carefully. The problem is that if the engine is continuing to over-fuel then the sensor will fail to switch, whether it's capable of doing so or not. Consequently, it must be 'fooled' into thinking that all is well so that it will resume its normal action, if at all possible. To do this, if you have a sensor producing a high voltage output ('go lean' signal because the mixture is too rich), disconnect one injector and effectively cut the fuel volume by 25%.

Instantly then the engine should go lean and, in turn, the Lambda sensor should switch to a low voltage output, signalling the ECU to send more fuel.

If it does not do this, or it takes ages to do so, then the sensor is definitely faulty. A replacement, at about £135, is the only solution. If this is necessary then think carefully about which replacement to buy. Non-original parts cost about half as much as OE versions, and Frank says that they will often be

Lambda sensor is tucked away on exhaust downpipe. Very awkward to get at.

the very same Bosch component. When you fit the sensor, you may well find that the earth reference is high. If this is the case then run a wire straight back to the battery's negative terminal to find the best possible earth. Ideally the value for this earth should be 0.2V or lower, preferably 0.1V.

One further pointer relating to the Lambda sensor is that, although it's very visible in the downpipe, actually locating a spanner to turn it is difficult. The problem is compounded by the fact that most will have seized in their mountings, and cannot be removed 'clean'. In such cases the downpipe has to be removed so that the thread can be cleared and the new sensor fitted. This can be a relatively time-consuming and expensive job.

On a similar note, there is another type of ECU problem which can lead to fuelling troubles. Frank has experienced this on a significant number of vehicles, and now recognises it as a characteristic failing. The symptoms are that the engine will be over-fuelling (alternatively of course, it might be under-fuelling) or, during serial communication operations, it will be impossible to bring fuelling within specification.

Quite often the cause will be the MAP sensor. It's likely to be operating out of range, but the degree of drift can be very subtle. It must be checked via serial communication and by using a vacuum gauge. Often these sorts of fault will be specific to a particular load range so, for example, trouble may only strike when the engine is cruising.

Faulty MAP sensors, because of their location within the ECU, are unrepairable so a replacement controller is the only practical solution. However, before

TECHNICAL SPECIFICATIONS

Component	Technical data
Stepper motor	12V to ground, frequency and duty modulation
Air temp sensor	3.5V cold, 2.5V hot
Coolant temp sensor	3.5V cold, 0.5V hot
Throttle potentiometer	5V reference plus earth 0.5V closed, 4.25V open
MAP sensor (within ECU)	Compare data from serial communications with vacuum readings
Oxygen sensor (four-wire)	Black wire 200-800mV switching at 1Hz minimum
Crank angle sensor	2V+ (peak to peak) cranking 11V idle 14V cruise
Injector duration	Cold idle – 3.5ms Hot idle – 2.5ms Snap load – 8-12ms Cold cranking – 8ms reducing to 4ms, followed by injector cut-off if cranking continues Hot cranking – 4ms

you finally condemn the ECU, fit it with a vacuum pump and check that the actual connecting pipe within the box has not been compromised. It must be capable of holding a good vacuum.

If it does leak away then there is obviously a problem within, but the good news is that the lid can be removed and the defective pipe renewed. The pipe can simply perish with age but also it can be damaged or dislodged if the outer extension on to which the vacuum pipe locates, gets broken off.

The ECU can also suffer with poor earths, leading to poor control functions for the injectors, stepper motor or even the coil. To check the earth references, Frank says that you really do need to employ an oscilloscope. A conventional multimeter may not be ac-

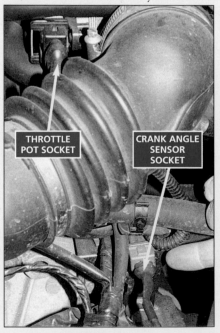

THROTTLE POT SOCKET

CRANK ANGLE SENSOR SOCKET

ROVER 214 1.4 DOHC
(Rover MEMS Mpi)

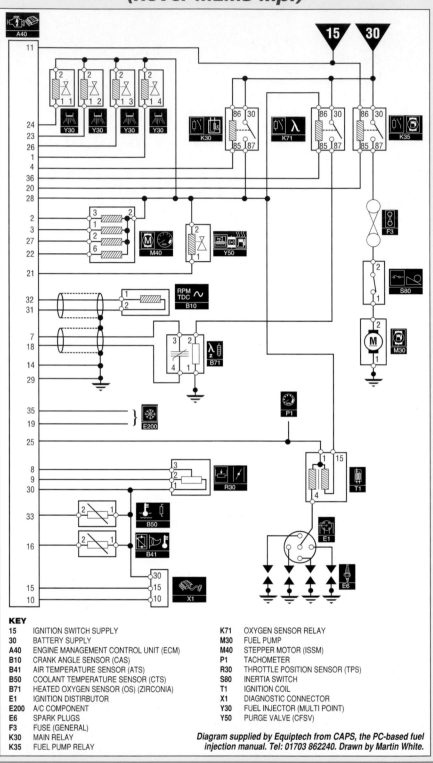

KEY

15	IGNITION SWITCH SUPPLY	K71	OXYGEN SENSOR RELAY
30	BATTERY SUPPLY	M30	FUEL PUMP
A40	ENGINE MANAGEMENT CONTROL UNIT (ECM)	M40	STEPPER MOTOR (ISSM)
B10	CRANK ANGLE SENSOR (CAS)	P1	TACHOMETER
B41	AIR TEMPERATURE SENSOR (ATS)	R30	THROTTLE POSITION SENSOR (TPS)
B50	COOLANT TEMPERATURE SENSOR (CTS)	S80	INERTIA SWITCH
B71	HEATED OXYGEN SENSOR (OS) (ZIRCONIA)	T1	IGNITION COIL
E1	IGNITION DISTIRBUTOR	X1	DIAGNOSTIC CONNECTOR
E200	A/C COMPONENT	Y30	FUEL INJECTOR (MULTI POINT)
E6	SPARK PLUGS	Y50	PURGE VALVE (CFSV)
F3	FUSE (GENERAL)		
K30	MAIN RELAY		
K35	FUEL PUMP RELAY		

Diagram supplied by Equiptech from CAPS, the PC-based fuel injection manual. Tel: 01703 862240. Drawn by Martin White.

curate enough to pick up odd electrical spikes or loadings on the circuit. Pin 29 is the main earth connection and any extra loadings on here can compromise component control.

If in any doubt, re-wire this pin directly to the negative battery terminal, and do the same for pin 30, which is the earth return for all the various sensors. If problems still persist then the ECU must be swapped.

One final point concerns the later encrypted systems, which use a totally different trigger signal. The phonic wheel (on the flywheel) has two cutouts; one for indicating TDC and the other for the encrypted alarm system. The ECUs from these models cannot be fitted to earlier cars without this system. Bear this in mind if you have swapped engines or ECUs and the motor won't start!

NEXT MONTH
Alarm faults fixed.

ELECTRONIC DIAGNOSTICS!

Tracing and fixing faults in electronic engine management systems

Number 58: *This month we're taking a general look at modern vehicle immobilisers and considering the problems being caused when they become faulty. Chris Graham reports.*

If you think that dealing with engine management failures on modern cars is difficult then sit down and pour yourself a stiff drink because it's nothing when compared to the complexity of rectifying troublesome engine immobilisers!

This really is a big growth area, in terms of faults reported, and is one where knowledge levels within the trade are worryingly low. Even at deal-ership level, understanding is often fragile and most in the trade are currently finding effective and economical problem-solving a real headache.

Part of the trouble is that these systems are so sensitive to mishandling. Indiscriminate component swapping can be a recipe for disaster.

Mike Walker, managing director of Staffordshire-based automotive electronics specialist ATP Electronic De-velopments Ltd (Tel: 01543 467466), sees first hand the problems being faced. He says: "We get phone calls on a daily basis now from technicians presented with alarm-related faults which they are unable to put right. The level of knowledge and appreciation of modern alarm system operation in the trade generally, even at the highest levels, is all but non-existent in my experience. Most dealerships will have a list

Key fob-activated security systems, either infra-red or radio based, are widely used today. Defects just starting to cause real problems.

SECURITY MANAGEMENT

Historically it was the insurance companies which prompted the vehicle manufacturers to get serious about car alarms and security. To begin with, car alarms were an afterthought as far as the vehicle manufacturers were concerned. Usually they were a dealer-fit option or, alternatively, were available for DIY fitting from the independent aftermarket.

The first systems offered by the original equipment manufacturers (OEMs) were little better than engineered-in versions of those already on sale through the trade. The immobiliser was a 'stand alone' fitting which typically did little more than break a circuit – usually the power feed to the starter motor.

Good examples of this are found on the early Rover 800, which features a couple of connectors behind the dashboard allowing installation of the unit.

Very low-tech and hardly secure against those who knew!

It wasn't until the early 1990s that manufacturers started making concerted efforts to secure vehicles effectively. But even then the good systems were restricted to range-topping models. Having wracked their collective brains for the best way forward, the motor industry decided it was best to integrate the immobiliser with the increasingly complex engine management systems being fitted. Disabling this provided the simplest and most effective way of preventing the engine from being started.

Early attempts were very basic. There was no clever internal electronics and here in lay the weakness. If you knew the pin number, you could disable the security system and start the engine.

At that stage manufacturers were reluctant to design more involved control systems simply because they feared that this would increase the risk of failure. So the simple approach remained for quite a while. A lot of GM vehicles, and BMWs of the mid and late 1980s, made use of such systems.

The next step saw an increase in signal sophistication. After initial power-up, the ECU was set to search for a specific signal and if none was found, then nothing would happen. This approach was adopted by Volkswagen and Vauxhall among others.

The most recent advance brings us to the current situation where a unique and often complex code is programmed into the engine management computer, relating specifically to the individual vehicle. The ECU will do nothing until it receives this code, by whatever means, and it is this approach which is now starting to cause serious repair problems.

Walker's general view is that: "The modern alarm systems, good though they undoubtedly are, will cause significant trouble in the future. Indeed they are doing so already. Because there is no way of beating the immobiliser, putting a faulty one right is a real problem. If an inherent part of the system fails, and fails in the 'no run' position, then you have problems!

"The complexity of the latest systems means that there are now more parts to go wrong, all capable of stopping the vehicle from running. This makes effective diagnosis tricky and the bill for doing so even greater. I believe these problems will start to have an influence on the resale value of cars as they begin to age."

of standard procedures to work through, but very few actually understand what is going on."

WHAT'S THE CODE?

Modern security systems rely completely on unique identification codes. Without them the ECU remains 'locked' and, in most cases, there is no way to get the engine started. This is why problems with the immobiliser system are so hard to overcome.

There are many different ways in which the code is presented to the main ECU and these all have their potential failings. One solution, used on Peugeot and Citroën models for example, is a simple keypad which the driver operates to input the multidigit security code. This is like using a cash machine requiring a PIN number – nothing happens until the correct number is entered.

On the face of it this is a sensible system, but there are associated problems which mean that its specification is being phased out. For a start all cars equipped with this system leave the factory with a default code setting. Owners, in some cases, never bother to alter this, which can give the budding thief an advantage straight away. He might discover that a particular model was always pre-programmed '1234', so this would naturally be tried first.

Fortunately, there is usually a limit to the number of attempts which can be made at the code. Typically a driver will get three chances to enter the correct number, after which the system will prevent another entry for 30 minutes. Then another three can be tried and, if still unsuccessful, the time delay doubles to an hour, and so on.

Another problem occurs if the code is forgotten, or if an owner maliciously changes it. The code can be changed as many times as necessary, but the previous one must be keyed in before a new one can be selected. There have been cases of disgruntled former employees resetting their company car codes as a final act of revenge!

Even a complete replacement can throw up problems, as Walker explains: "We have found that the keypads suffer with age. Most feature tinned copper circuit boards with tiny connectors which, through lack of use, become dirty. If the same code is retained for several years the keys not being used become tarnished and ineffective.

"Having to log in the default code for the replacement system can prove impossible, with the faulty keys generating spurious outputs and leaving the main ECU decidedly unimpressed!" To avoid this sort of problem the solution is to vary the security code at regular intervals, using as many different numbers as possible, so that all are used relatively frequently. On the plus side of things, the keypad-based system works independently of the ignition key. So even if a thief gets his hands on the ignition key, he still will not be able to start the engine unless he gets lucky with the code. With most other alternative systems, if he gets hold of the key he is home and dry!

Another common approach is to link the immobiliser directly to the central locking system. The controller for this is programmed with the car's security code so that when the key triggers the door lock, the magic numbers are squirted off to

Keypad provides a simple way of inputting the vehicle security code needed to unlock the immobiliser on Peugeot and Citroën models.

84

ELECTRONIC DIAGNOSTICS!

Body control computer and controlling key fob – perhaps the most secure system yet.

the main ECU to prepare the engine for action.

Rover and Renault have made much use of this approach and it works well. However, ATP's Mike Walker has his reservations. He says: "The nature of this set-up means that if anything goes wrong there is a lot of componentry to be replaced.

"But the biggest disadvantage is that to override the system requires nothing more than triggering the central locking mechanism. As long as the central locking computer can be activated, the rest of the immobiliser system will follow. This system is no more secure than a good key."

RADIO TIMES!

Another even more modern security solution is for the vehicle to be fitted with what Walker describes as a 'body control computer'. This is basically the heart of the car. If it's not working then nothing else will!

A common way of activating this unit is by using key fob control. A security code is sent by a radio transmitter in the fob, to a receiver located somewhere on the vehicle. Once the body computer is triggered by this it 'wakes up' the rest of the car, unlocking the doors and preparing the engine management system for operation.

This is a very secure system, particularly when combined with transmission locks etc. The big disadvantage is that any problems with it cause great inconvenience. Something as simple as a flat battery in the key fob means the car will be undriveable – even the correct door key used manually will be useless.

Key fobs like this are relatively vulnerable and should not be thrown about, dropped, trodden on etc. Problems can also arise with other radio interference which overpowers the fob transmitter.

The alternative version of this system relies on an infra-red signal instead of radio waves. Usually this will be set to trigger the central locking computer, rather than transmitting directly to the main engine management ECU or body computer.

The latest preferred method is to use a key-borne transponder system, in which the ignition key body contains a tiny antenna and microchip. There is no power requirement so no battery is needed.

A coil of wire is fitted around the ignition lock barrel and this is energised by power from the ignition when the key is initially turned. This generates enough of a signal to power-up the key-based chip, which is then encouraged to divulge its stored security code. A second coil of wire around the lock barrel, this time a signal receiver, senses this tiny broadcast and, assuming all is well, passes it on directly to the engine computer to power up the system allowing the engine to be started.

Walker says: "This is the preferred method these days simply because it is so user-friendly. It's other significant advantage over the 'radio' approach is that it is very safe. There have been instances where criminals will use a radio scanner to intercept and record security code signals for later use.

THE SEQUENCE GAME

"Also, the fact that the key-mounted chip requires no battery is a big plus point, and it is a robust unit too. The most common cause of problems is a lost key. Usually the owner will have to return to the dealer with proof of ownership (quoting the car's VIN number) so that a replacement key can be programmed and issued. This normally takes several days."

A further refinement of the system features a so called 'rolling code', which uses a different security number

Modern keys feature a tiny microchip (left) built into the handle. The key takes its power from an inductive coil fitted around the ignition lock barrel (top).

each time the immobiliser is operated. This is changed, by the car-based computer and the key, according to a sequence which is pre-programmed into both. Repetition does eventually occur, but the sequence can be very long. So, simply copying the key and the code it contains at that time will achieve nothing because the car will demand a new one the next time it is unlocked. Each successive code is completely different so it's not simply a matter of increasing the existing number by one digit.

Walker warns: "One potential problem is that repeated pressing of the fob button, while in a pocket for example, will progress its sequence on a step at a time. So that when the system is next used for real, it and the sequence stored in the car may well be out of step. Fortunately, the car side of things has the capability to look ahead in the sequence and recognise if successive numbers have been skipped. But there is a limit to this, so don't let your children play with the key fob!"

Another form of rolling code system uses the same general principal but features the ability not only to vary the security numbers, but also the sequence in which they are used. This is perhaps the ultimate in security terms because there isn't a single sequence with a beginning and an end, which is repeated. Instead the system has the capability to re-write the sequence at any time.

According to Walker, Fiat have adopted this system across their entire model range. He says: "When you buy a new vehicle it is supplied with a red key and two blue keys. The red one not only contains the data to operate the system, but also embodies the master encryption data which sets the sequence pattern.

This data is not held in the blue keys,

so duplicates can only be made from the red master key. If the red key is missing you will need new door locks, new keys, new immobiliser unit and a new ECU."

MISSION IMPOSSIBLE?

These all-singing, all-dancing immobiliser systems are no longer the preserve of the prestigious flagship models. In the past two years the most complex alarm systems have worked their way down through most model ranges. This means that the problems they suffer with will have to be considered by us all, sooner or later. In my opinion, the troubles we are seeing now represent just the tip of a very nasty and technically involved iceberg!

At present it's impossible to be specific about the most common causes of system failure – it really is too early to say. Walker explains: "We have certainly seen all the typical water-related and design-prompted failures but, in some cases it really is not clear what has caused the fault."

Effective diagnosis of these defects is very difficult in many instances. Even determining whether or not the problem is alarm-related can be a job in itself. Some cars, such as Vauxhalls, make life a little easier by giving the dash-mounted engine management light a dual role. It is flashed rapidly to denote an immobiliser-related fault. But remember this only provides a very general guide, giving no help about the actual cause of the fault.

Unfortunately, many other cars provide no clue at all about the nature of the problem – everything simply goes dead. Most can be interrogated to a certain extent by dealer-issue code reading equipment but this is limited. The situation is not helped by the fact that commonly, diagnostic equipment is designed to be used while the engine is running.

If you have a car which is inexplicably failing to start, the first thing to establish is whether or not there is even an immobiliser fitted to the vehicle. If there is, you must then decide what sort it is and how it's operated.

PROBLEM SOLVING

If it is key-operated then do you have the correct key? Try to find out the history of the fault. It's amazing how many people continue to waste time by not asking questions of the owner. If the vehicle has been bought from an auction, for example, then all sorts of components may have been swapped before the sale.

Establish the circumstances immediately prior to the failure and, if the handbook is with the car, read it carefully. If you have a fault code reader for the vehicle see if this can be used to check for immobiliser faults without the engine running.

Resist the temptation to swap the ECU with an 'off the shelf' replacement, unless you are very confident about what you are doing. If the immobiliser system is generating erratic outputs and these were responsible for scrambling the original unit, successive replacements will be ruined in the same way until the root cause is rectified.

Walker adds: "Don't forget that the problem may be being caused by something as simple as a flat battery in the key fob. Normally the range of operation of the key transmitter will get shorter and shorter as the battery loses power.

The owner should have noticed this so consultation with him/her could prove invaluable.

"Never rush into repairs and never start swapping components without being sure of your ground. The best advice may often be to get the vehicle to the nearest main dealer so that dedicated code reading equipment can be used for an initial assessment."

He explains: "We at ATP can test an ECU to establish whether the fault lies with it rather than with the immobiliser. Or whether the ECU has been corrupted by input from the immobiliser controller. Unfortunately, there is no simple way of testing most immobiliser systems to isolate a fault."

Another possible option is that ATP are able to supply a replacement ECU which will disarm the immobiliser system completely, and allow the car to run. All security devices will be inoperative, of course, but on older, less valuable vehicles this may prove to be the most sensible way forward.

In other cases problem cars can be fitted with ATP self-programming units. These will read the immobiliser data, programme themselves to it and then allow the car to function quite normally.

So the overall story is not particularly encouraging. There's trouble on the horizon and sorting it out is sure to prove time-consuming and expensive for all but the best equipped specialists. We hope to return to this complex subject later in the series with some typical case studies illustrating the diagnosis and rectification of the most commonly occurring immobiliser faults.

NEXT MONTH
MINI COOPER

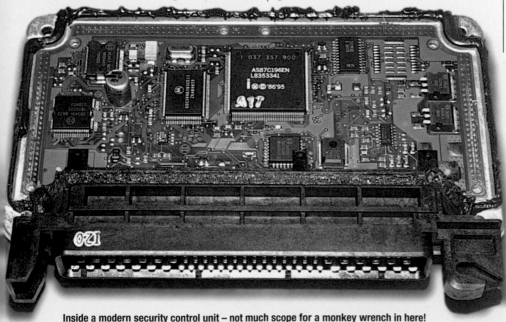

Inside a modern security control unit – not much scope for a monkey wrench in here!

ELECTRONIC DIAGNOSTICS!

Tracing and fixing faults in electronic engine management systems

Number 59: Finally we've got round to covering a Mini! Chris Graham reports on some of the problems likely to afflict this pint-sized box of tricks.

Thanks mainly to tightening safety regulations, Mini, as we know it, is into its final year of production and, engine-wise has reached perhaps the limit of its technological potential. The heart of the motor is still the trusty old A Series engine albeit festooned with many of the most up-to-date additions which Rover has to offer.

Frank Massey, our guiding light on all things electronic, and proprietor of

Preston-based Fuel Injection Services (Tel: 01772 201597), is not the greatest Mini fan in the UK but was, nevertheless, keen to have a closer look at the gleaming new Cooper we presented for his expert consideration.

The electronic brains behind the latest Mini Cooper is the most recent version of MEMS (Modular Engine Management System), denoted simply as MEMS 2J. Added to this, Rover have finally broken away from the, at times, asthmatic single-point fuel injection system, and developed a variation on the multipoint theme. Frank would actually classify this as 'dualpoint' rather than multipoint, simply because there are only two fuel injectors.

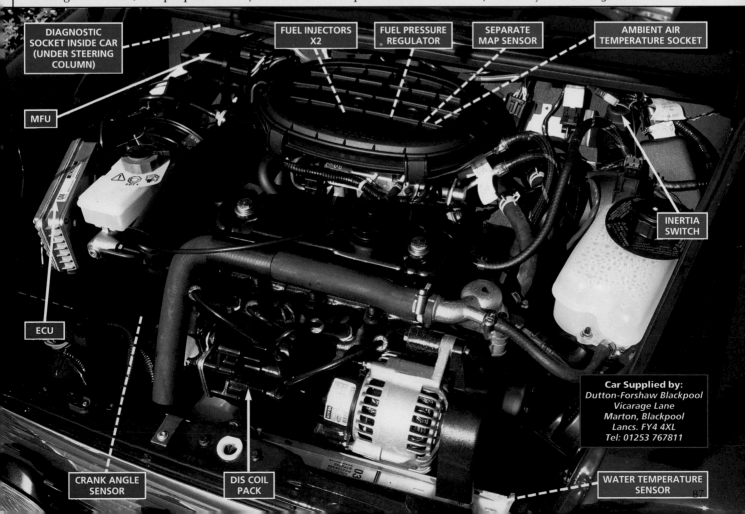

DIAGNOSTIC SOCKET INSIDE CAR (UNDER STEERING COLUMN)

FUEL INJECTORS X2

FUEL PRESSURE REGULATOR

SEPARATE MAP SENSOR

AMBIENT AIR TEMPERATURE SOCKET

MFU

INERTIA SWITCH

ECU

CRANK ANGLE SENSOR

DIS COIL PACK

WATER TEMPERATURE SENSOR

Car Supplied by:
*Dutton-Forshaw Blackpool
Vicarage Lane
Marton, Blackpool
Lancs. FY4 4XL
Tel: 01253 767811*

87

ENGINE MANAGEMENT

This version of MEMS arrived early in 1997 and so it's still early days to be specific about problems.

The system is essentially straightforward and features DIS ignition, making use of the 'wasted spark' approach to firing the plugs. This represents a big improvement as Minis historically suffered from the old-fashioned distributor's forward location at the front of the engine.

The component layout, with regard to engine management, is pretty much conventional. The two injectors are fed from a single fuel rail with a pressure regulator at one end. Other major components include: a water temperature sensor built into the thermostat housing; an idle control stepper motor; a charcoal canister and purge valve for dealing with tank fumes.

An ambient air temperature sensor in the air intake manifold; an inertia switch found under the bonnet on the n/s rear bulkhead; the aforementioned dual ignition coil which is driven directly by the ECU; a MAP sensor mounted on the inlet manifold – no rubber hose to worry about.

There is a throttle position sensor; a crank angle sensor, at the back of the bell housing; a camshaft sensor and a four-wire Lambda sensor, running 'closed loop' control on the exhaust emissions.

The fuel pump is mounted within the petrol tank which, in effect, is in the boot. The main relays take the form of a single, multi-function unit (MFU) which combines four relays in the one component. It includes a main relay, a fuel pump relay, an oxygen sensor relay and a starter relay. Because of its construction, the MFU can only be changed as one unit.

There is a 16-pin J1962 diagnostic socket found under the dashboard. This provides access to fault codes, enables live data to be recorded and allows actuators to be driven for testing purposes. There is also a full vehicle immobiliser fitted. This is an integral system and should never be overlooked as a possible cause of trouble.

Multipoint generally refers to a set-up with one injector per cylinder. In this case, each injector is mounted in a Siamese port and features two outlet nozzles aligned at about 30° to each other. However, all other attributes you would expect to find with a full-blown multipoint system are present here.

Generally, Frank is impressed with the quality of the installation, although he admits that space is at a premium. The ECU is easy to get at, being located at the front of the engine bay on the o/s inner wing. Its socket is positioned on the underside of the unit but, despite this precaution, Frank still thinks that water ingress might be a problem in the future.

PREPARATION

The first rule to remember when dealing with this engine is that its design is an old one and so often the cause of faults can be mechanical in nature. The A Series unit still relies on mechanical pushrods, rocker shaft and rockers. Don't assume that just because this application appears to bristle with electronic control systems, that every problem will be ECU, wiring or sensor-related.

Mechanical adjustments are still vital and all settings should be checked to eliminate the obvious before wading into complex electronic diagnostics. For example, errors in the setting of the tappets can have a very significant effect on the switching of the Lambda sensor.

The air cleaner is very easy to remove and check, so always do this as part of your routine preparation procedure. The ambient air temperature sensor is no longer found within this housing, so this simplifies the checking operation.

The engine features a very simple down-draught throttle body, made largely of plastic. Frank believes that this may well be in an attempt to reduce the risk of icing-up. Carefully wash this out using a good quality carburettor cleaner spray.

The spark plugs are simplicity itself to access and check. As always, remove them all and inspect each carefully for signs of abnormal appearance – unusual discoloration or oiling etc. Check the gaps and that the plugs themselves are the right type. Also, watch out for 'corona rings' around the base of the ceramic body sections.

These will take the form of obvious brownish yellow staining and provide conclusive evidence that electrical tracking is occurring down the plug lead. The DIS ignition used on this car means that it's running a high powered HT system – up to 60,000V – and so problems with the leads will dramatically promote the likelihood of tracking. Remember, as well, that the leads face towards the front of the car and so will catch any road dirt or moisture going. Remove the leads and wash them. Check each carefully for cracks and splits and make sure all are clean and dry before re-fitting.

Incidentally, the brand new car we photographed here sported a set of leads which were covered in a 'beautifying' lacquer. Frank says that, as time passes, this type of product ages and alters character to create a wonderfully effective electrical conductivity path – not the best prospect in the world! Consequently, he would far rather see plug leads left untreated, clean and dry. His advice is to remove such treatments and, if you can't, then scrap the leads and buy a new set. They won't break the bank but will ensure reliable service.

Finally, run a fault code check as part of your basic preparation procedure. Extract any stored faults using a code reader, note them and then clear the lot. Drive the car and check which, if any, return. Remember that some may well have been induced by nothing more suspicious than a mechanic disconnecting sockets during some previous service or repair operations. Any which do return should be treated as faults and marked down for further investigation.

MINI MINUSES

The problem we face here is that this version of the Mini is still a relatively new car and so faults are comparatively rare. But Frank's extensive experience with the marque over the years, together with his knowledge of the

Simple throttle body made primarily from plastic.

ELECTRONIC DIAGNOSTICS!

Rover MEMS management system, means he is able to predict some of the most likely troubles in store.

The first potential problem he came up with relates to bad earths. The battery in the Mini is found in the boot, so the earth references have to travel the entire length of the car to reach the negative battery terminal. As with most modern engine management systems, the quality of the earth references is crucial for smooth operation. Frank says that many of the sensors reference the voltage quite close to pure ground, particularly the Lambda sensor. Because of this there is always a potential for earth-related problems.

The symptoms of these can be many and varied, including high throttle potentiometer voltage, poor Lambda switching (where it's not ranging completely down), lean mixture caused by poor injector switching, loss of idle control or a misfiring engine, among others. There is, of course, significant danger of miss-diagnosis. It's easy to jump to the wrong conclusion, blaming either the components of even the ECU, for this problem.

Traditionally there has often been problems with a particular earth return on the offside of the vehicle's bulkhead – the MEMS unit itself returns to this point. The reference has then to travel back through the Mini's body to reach the battery, and down its cable which is bolted to the chassis.

When you check earths they have to be in a 'loaded' condition (ie with a running engine, or one being cranked). Static checks are simply not adequate. A good earth reference would be a maximum of 200mV (0.2V), according to Frank. If this rises to more than 0.5V when the engine's being cranked, then you're starting to get into the problem zone when trouble can strike.

There are no short cuts when dealing with earth problems. The wires

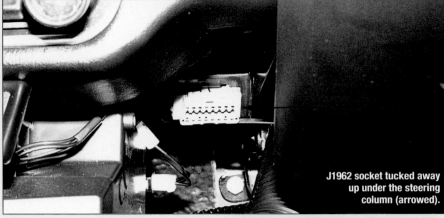

J1962 socket tucked away up under the steering column (arrowed).

must be removed so that the chassis areas can be dressed using an angle grinder. Achieving a bare metal finish is vital, after which a rust inhibitor should be applied – Frank says Vaseline is as good as anything for this. Also, check the earth tabs on the wires and, if necessary, tin-solder them. Often these days they will simply have been crimped at the factory, which can be a source of trouble. If in doubt, re-terminate completely.

In the boot of the car, remove the main earth strap from the chassis and make sure it has a good, bare-metal contact too. Often, Frank says, you find these mounted straight on to paint so the system is relying on thread contact which, quite often, simply isn't good enough. Grind away the paint here as well, if necessary. Also, you might find it advisable in some cases to install additional earth circuits. Frank has done this a number of times by soldering on an additional earth loom and running it from the affected component to a new earth point elsewhere on the chassis.

Frank emphasises the importance of good earth connections, and says that checking them should always be a priority with any engine or management system which is not performing as it should.

Another potential cause of trouble on this application is the crank angle sensor (CAS). This provides the primary input to the ECU and its efficient performance is crucial. Its location, within the bell housing, makes it vulnerable to contamination from metallic dust created as the starter ring gear wears. The

sensor is magnetic and so attracts this sort of debris. In time the build-up of material on the sensor body will start to have an adverse effect on the quality of the signal it produces, leading to driveability problems, including misfires, then eventually engine failure.

The 'shape' of the sensor's output signal (as viewed on an oscilloscope) is vital, as far as the ECU is concerned. If it becomes distorted by a defect, including metallic contamination, problems are sure to occur. The simplest way to check for this condition is to assess the output signal profile using an oscilloscope.

If it's discovered that any part of the signal trace is miss-shapen, then the chances are that the sensor is at fault. However, don't automatically assume this without checking first. The problem may also be mechanical in nature. Trouble with the phonic wheel, which is bolted on to the flywheel and provides the signal input for the crank angle sensor, can have the same result. The wheel can be damaged during

CRANK ANGLE SENSOR PROBLEMS?

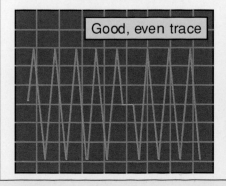

Good, even trace

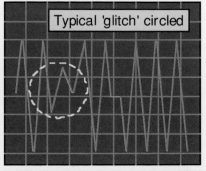

Typical 'glitch' circled

careless repair work, for example. Bear this in mind if you get a car in with mysterious running problems.

Frank had a typical example in recently, where the car was running, but badly. It appeared to be over-fuelling because the Lambda sensor was not switching and the plugs were visibly sooty. Yet, despite carrying out a thorough assessment of the complete engine management system, no fault could be found. In fact, the only oddity at all was that the ignition timing point was incredibly advanced – by about 60°! The most likely causes of this were a problem with the ECU or a fault with the triggering mechanism. He eliminated the control unit as a cause, only then to find that the trigger signal from the crank angle sensor was good also, so this couldn't be faulted either.

Following a consultation with the dealership which had referred the car, it was discovered that the engine had been running perfectly up until a clutch change (undertaken by a rapid-fit centre!). Knowing this, Frank was immediately suspicious of the phonic wheel and, closer inspection revealed

that it was not bolted correctly to the flywheel. The securing bolt layout means that it is possible to attach this important component in three different positions, although just one is correct. The two wrong positions give ignition which is advanced or retarded by a whopping 60°!

The catch is, that apart from the poor performance, everything else appeared fine. Even the trace on the oscilloscope looked perfect! This particular car arrived with Frank from a Rover main dealer, who ran into a diagnostic brick wall because they were looking at the problem electronically and had not considered the mechanical possibilities.

Finally, Frank thinks there's a possibility of fuel injector problems with this vehicle as mileage builds. Because there are only two injectors supplying the fuel for four cylinders, he believes that each employs a split nozzle arrangement. For this reason the likelihood of trouble is increased. A partial blockage in one or other of the nozzles causes a corresponding increase in flow through the remaining one. This then sets up a fuelling imbalance be-

tween those two cylinders.

The evidence of this can be seen clearly at the spark plugs. Any which looks out of place will point towards an injector-related problem with that cylinder. Another potential problem can arise if manifold bolts are not tight. This can result in a loss of pressure and driveability problems. Any air leaks on the inlet side will allow in additional oxygen that will be detected by the Lambda sensor, which, in turn, will lean off the mixture accordingly.

An air leak on the exhaust side is potentially even more critical, because this will allow oxygen in after combustion has taken place which will certainly lead to over-fuelling. This will be irrespective of the original mixture quality.

Faulty injectors should be removed and tested professionally using a flow bench so that spray patterns and delivery rates can be assessed accurately. If they do not respond to cleaning then replacement is the only solution.

NEXT MONTH
RENAULT MEGANE

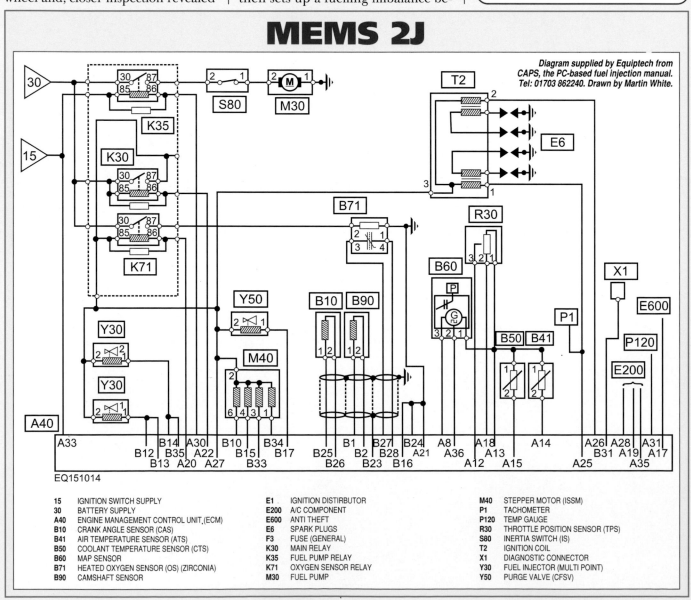

MEMS 2J

Diagram supplied by Equiptech from CAPS, the PC-based fuel injection manual. Tel: 01703 862240. Drawn by Martin White.

EQ151014

15	IGNITION SWITCH SUPPLY	**E1**	IGNITION DISTIRBUTOR	**M40**	STEPPER MOTOR (ISSM)
30	BATTERY SUPPLY	**E200**	A/C COMPONENT	**P1**	TACHOMETER
A40	ENGINE MANAGEMENT CONTROL UNIT (ECM)	**E600**	ANTI THEFT	**P120**	TEMP GAUGE
B10	CRANK ANGLE SENSOR (CAS)	**E6**	SPARK PLUGS	**R30**	THROTTLE POSITION SENSOR (TPS)
B41	AIR TEMPERATURE SENSOR (ATS)	**F3**	FUSE (GENERAL)	**S80**	INERTIA SWITCH (IS)
B50	COOLANT TEMPERATURE SENSOR (CTS)	**K30**	MAIN RELAY	**T2**	IGNITION COIL
B60	MAP SENSOR	**K35**	FUEL PUMP RELAY	**X1**	DIAGNOSTIC CONNECTOR
B71	HEATED OXYGEN SENSOR (OS) (ZIRCONIA)	**K71**	OXYGEN SENSOR RELAY	**Y30**	FUEL INJECTOR (MULTI POINT)
B90	CAMSHAFT SENSOR	**M30**	FUEL PUMP	**Y50**	PURGE VALVE (CFSV)

ELECTRONIC DIAGNOSTICS!

Tracing and fixing faults in electronic engine management systems

Number 60: Chris Graham gets to grips with Renault's stylish yet practical Renault Megane Scenic.

The car we've picked this month is the Tardis-like Renault Megane Scenic – tiny looking from the outside but surprisingly spacious within! The model here is powered by the 1.6-litre engine, designated K7M, which is a popular choice.

The 'brains' behind the car are provided by a Siemens electronic control unit running Renault's own Fenix 5 management system, which was first introduced at the end of 1996. The ECU is a 55-pin unit and is mounted

vertically under the bonnet, on the o/s of the engine bay. Fenix 5 in this guise runs with multi-point fuel injection, which is semi-sequential. This means that the injectors are fired in pairs.

For some expert comment about this car's workshop manners we consulted independent electronic diagnostics guru Simon Ashby whose company Diagnostic Technique (Tel: 07971 300481) carrys out product testing for the likes of Sykes-Pickavant and Equiptech.

Overall, Simon is an admirer of the Fenix 5 system. He considers it to be efficient, generally reliable and of reasonable quality. Installation is to a high standard but, despite this, some characteristic failure points are already starting to become apparent.

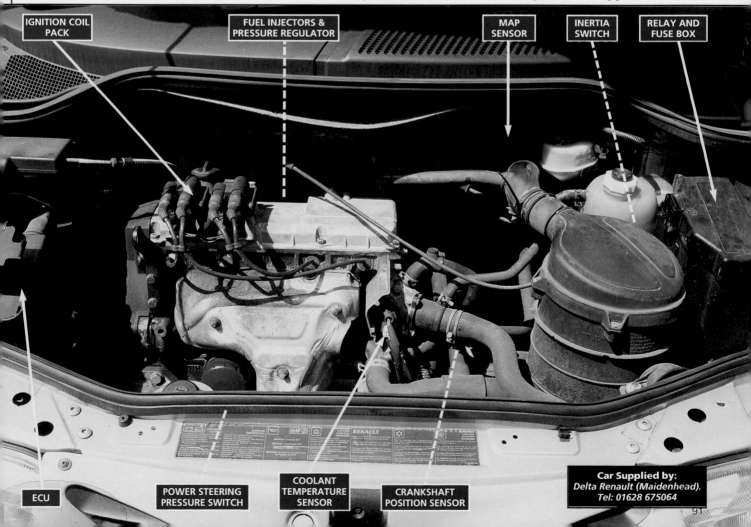

IGNITION COIL PACK

FUEL INJECTORS & PRESSURE REGULATOR

MAP SENSOR

INERTIA SWITCH

RELAY AND FUSE BOX

ECU

POWER STEERING PRESSURE SWITCH

COOLANT TEMPERATURE SENSOR

CRANKSHAFT POSITION SENSOR

Car Supplied by:
Delta Renault (Maidenhead).
Tel: 01628 675064

89

ENGINE MANAGEMENT

This system is relatively straightforward in terms of layout and content. Ignition is supplied in the modern way, using a coil pack, containing two coils, which operates on the 'wasted spark' principal. This is a very reliable system, primarily because there are no moving parts to wear out, but it does eventually fail, as we'll see later.

The significant components within the system consist of: a knock sensor, positioned at the rear of the engine block and beneath the inlet manifold, which makes access difficult; an air temperature sensor; a TDC sensor for denoting engine position and phasing fuel injection and ignition timing; a coolant temperature sensor.

There's also a power steering pressure switch which increases engine idle speed to compensate to power steering operation; a MAP sensor providing the primary system input to the ECU; a throttle potentiometer for registering throttle position; an idle speed control stepper motor and a three-wire Lambda sensor which is heated.

There are main and fuel relays, both located under the bonnet within a plastic box on the n/s of the engine bay; four conventional fuel injectors; an inertia switch found under the bonnet (red cap); a fuel pump located inside the tank, with a separate filter just in front of the tank.

All cars are supplied with a factory-fitted engine immobiliser system. This is overridden by locking and unlocking the doors.

If the car is left for more than about a minute with the ignition off then the immobiliser kicks in, signified by a rapidly flashing red LED in the centre of the dash. While this is flashing the engine will not run.

There is a 16-pin J1962 diagnostic socket located behind a trim panel low down on the dashboard, to the right of the steering column. Simon says that at present the DIY diagnostic prospects are limited for this vehicle. But we gather from Sykes-Pickavant that their excellent Advanced Code Reader will soon have the capability to deal with this Fenix system. Currently the best results are achieved using Renault's own XR25 diagnostic test machine. This provides access to fault codes and live data.

PREPARATION

As far as Simon's concerned, this particular Renault engine application doesn't suffer too badly from dirt contamination. The car featured here has covered just 36,000 miles and the engine is visibly dirty, but Simon does not think this a problem. He says that the Megane suffers no more than any other modern car which is not fitted with an undertray beneath the engine.

One of the first things that Simon checks on this system is the correct functioning of the vehicle's factory-fitted immobiliser. This is a crucial factor and is something which should never be overlooked in a 'no run' situation.

Under normal conditions, once the ignition has been switched on, the immobiliser warning LED in the centre of the dash will be extinguished after about three seconds – at the same time as the engine fault indicator light. The vehicle can then be started. However, if the light flashes rapidly then this indicates that the immobiliser is active, preventing the engine from running. Bear this in mind if you've been carrying out work only to find that the engine will not re-start!

It's wise also to check fuel pressures and delivery rates if you're dealing with a power-related problem, and also to inspect the spark plugs. These must be of the correct type and be set with appropriate gaps.

Don't ignore the basics either. Assess the electrical system, making sure that there's a spark at all four outlets from the twin coil pack. 'Distributorless' coils can sometimes be at the root of driveability problems, so it's well worth spending a little time checking for faults at the preparation stage.

Routine maintenance checks, such as inspecting the air filter, all rubber hoses, cam timing etc, are vital too. The latter can be a crucial factor and

problems with it can be the source of many an apparently baffling fault. As Simon says, cars which 'hunt' at idle but perform perfectly at all other speeds, can be suffering in this way.

It's easy to discount the cambelt, or alternatively, reject checking it simply because it's an awkward, time-consuming job. The other unfortunate tendency is to wrongly assume that all engine performance-related faults with modern cars must be electrical in nature, disregarding the basics.

Diagnostic socket found under a black cap, behind a trim panel to the right of the steering column.

One thing worth checking carefully is the condition of the rocker cover gasket. These have been modified in recent times and a metal version is now standard fit. Before this a paper type was used, which was rather prone to leaks. Signs of oil seepage around this joint should be regarded with suspicion.

Finally, talk to the vehicle owner whenever possible. Learning something of the car's recent history can be tremendously valuable. Information about the nature of the fault, or work which has been carried out in the recent past, will often provide precious clues enabling you to narrow down your search, thus saving time and money.

DEALING WITH TROUBLE

Although the Renault Megane is essentially a very good and reliable motor car, there are already a number of characteristic failings which it's important to be aware of. The first of these relates to sensor corrosion.

In this case, the component most commonly affected is the coolant tem-

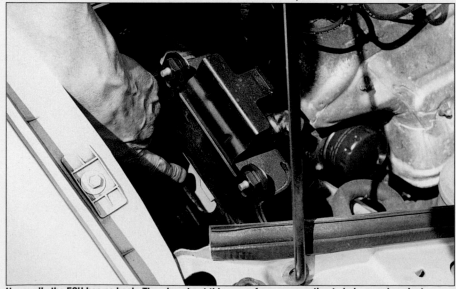
Unusually the ECU has no back. Theories about this range from a precaution to help guard against overheating to a cost-saving measure taken by the manufacturer.

perature sensor. If you're presented with a car which starts badly from cold and is reluctant to rev before the engine has warmed, then a likely cause is a rotted sensor. The potentially confusing factor is that performance and starting ability returns to normal once the engine is up to its correct operating temperature.

The problem is caused by the fact that the sensor is failing, or has failed, and consequently, the ECU is being sent a constantly high voltage output indicating that the engine is already thoroughly warmed. The result of this is that fuelling is reduced creating initial starting and running problems.

This type of fault may be insufficiently severe to trigger the dashboard warning light, or to log and store a fault code within the system, despite its serious effect on engine performance. However, it will be picked up with a diagnostic tool which can be used to check sensor outputs.

The root of this problem is a simple lack of antifreeze/coolant additive. Without an adequate concentration of this essential additive in the coolant solution, there will be little or no resistance to corrosion and the coolant sensor will be one of the first components to suffer.

A quick visual check of the coolant's appearance in the header tank should tell you a lot. Liquid that appears brown and even frothy is likely to contain very little coolant additive. If this

Tucked up against the bulkhead, at the back of the engine bay, you'll find the idle speed control motor (A) and the MAP sensor (B). Also here, but hidden from view behind the stepper motor, is the throttle position indicator switch.

is the case then remove the sensor itself – a simple case of unscrewing it – and inspect its body carefully. If corrosion is the problem it will usually be self evident from this visual examination.

Rectification will involve flushing the coolant system and replacing the fluid, together with the recommended concentration of additive, followed by fitting a new sensor. Simon advises that replacements are relatively cheap – costing about £20 – and emphasises the importance of fitting a new sealing washer and ensuring that antifreeze concentrations are correctly maintained throughout the year. Many drivers tend to forget all about this once the weather warms, but the corrosion inhibitors in modern coolant additives make their presence a year-round essential.

COIL PACK FAILURE

Another typical fault relates to the coil pack. It's quite common for one or other of the coil ends to fail for no apparent reason. These components tend to break down at random, rather like a light bulb. One minute they're working, the next they're not!

It's rare for both to fail at the same time, but when one goes the engine will obviously be reduced to two cylinders. Simon has seen this on many occasions on cars which have been driven to his workshop by their owners who are complaining about an extreme lack of power. Using the car in this condition is not a good idea. Not only is there potential for engine damage, but the unburnt fuel pumped through the system will play havoc with the catalytic converter in the exhaust.

On some occasions there will be visible signs of electrical tracking on the

outside of the coil body, but usually the presence of the problem will have to be detected by conventional testing. Before jumping to any conclusions, check first that there's an output signal from the control unit. A 12-volt ignition feed is essential for correct operation. Also, look around for any other signs of obvious damage and check that all the plug leads are properly connected.

If you're sure that one half of the coil pack is faulty, then the good news is that the 'halves' can be replaced on an individual basis. Simon is quite happy to recommend the replacement of these units one at a time because he says that the failure of one provides no indication about the condition of the

Inertia switch found in the engine. Normally this device will only be triggered by an impact, but it's possible that accidentally knocking it during clutch changing operations could trip it, preventing the engine from being started until the switch is reset.

other. He's not aware of a practical service life for these units and adds that replacements cost about £50 each.

The third common failing on this system centres around a short section of loom found low down in the engine bay on the n/s of the vehicle. Here a length of it loops down under the gearbox and passes very close to the vehicle's subframe. In many cases, due to engine movement, the two will come into contact, and with time the protective armour, then the insulation, will be worn through.

Once bare wires have been exposed, all sorts of short-circuiting occurs, sometimes with serious consequences, but other times simply resulting in niggly faults. Usually these problems will start intermittently, but as the loom's condition worsens they will become permanent and will often be sufficient to prevent the engine from running. Such problems will also be exacerbated by damp or wet conditions – this area

being particularly exposed to road splash.

It's always worth checking this area of the loom and any problems will be self-evident, either visually or by feel. The method chosen for putting this problem right rather depends on the severity of the damage. Simon advises

that if the chafing is limited to the insulation, then simple taping up to create a watertight seal will be sufficient.

But if the problem has been serious enough to cause overheating and melting of the wires then you may have to consider replacing the damaged lengths. This is not an easy job and should only be attempted by those experienced in this type of work. For the binding-up type of repairs Simon chooses to use a product called Self Amalgamating Tape. This is a material which only sticks to itself, so is easy to handle but very effective at creating a water and dirt-tight covering as well as complete electrical insulation.

Finally, of course, the repaired section of loom should be tied back away from the subframe to prevent the same thing happening again.

NEXT MONTH
Citroën Saxo 1.6

TECHNICAL SPECIFICATIONS

Lambda sensor	Output ranges from 0-1V
Fuel injectors	12V supply
	Resistance 14.5 ohms approx
	Duration 3-3.2ms approx
Fuel pressure	3 bar without vacuum
	2.5 bar with vacuum
Air temp. sensor	7-11K @ 0°C
	1.3-1.6K @ 40°C
Coolant temp. sensor	3-4K @ 20°C
	210-270 ohms @ 90°C
Throttle pos. sensor	200 ohms
Idle speed	750rpm
Coil pack	Primary resistance 1 ohm or less
	Secondary resistance 10K

(Note: K = 1,000 ohms)

FENIX 5

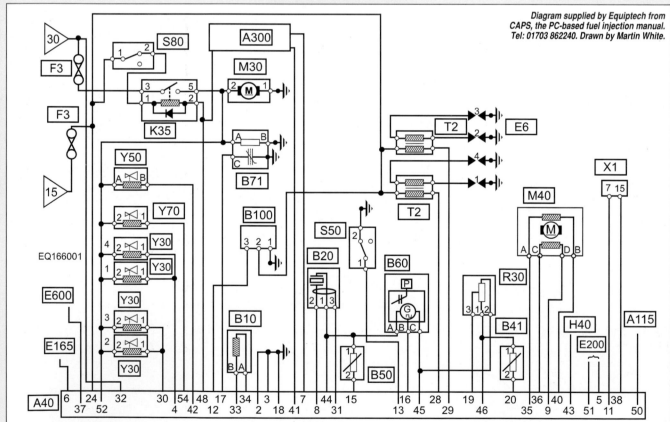

Diagram supplied by Equiptech from CAPS, the PC-based fuel injection manual. Tel: 01703 862240. Drawn by Martin White.

15	Ignition switch supply	**B60**	MAP Sensor (analogue)
30	Battery supply	**B71**	Heated Lambda Sensor (zirconia)
A115	Instrument cluster	**E165**	Heated Rear Window
A300	Automatic Transmission Control Unit	**E200**	A/C component
A40	Engine management control unit	**E6**	Spark plugs
B10	Engine Position and Speed Sensor	**E600**	Anti Theft
B100	Vehicle Speed Sensor	**F3**	Fuse (general)
B20	Knock Sensor	**H40**	Engine Management Warning Lamp
B41	Air Temperature Sensor	**K35**	Fuel Pump Relay
B50	Coolant Temperature Sensor	**M30**	Fuel Pump

M40	Stepper Motor
R30	Throttle Position Sensor
S50	Power Steering Pressure Switch
S80	Inertia Switch
T2	Distributorless ignition coil (wasted spark)
X01	Self Diagnosis connector
Y30	Fuel injector (Multi point)
Y50	Purge Valve
Y70	EGR solenoid valve

on
Electronic Diagnostics

Volume 3